SELMA EVANS

WOMEN WITH ADHD

EFFECTIVE STRATEGIES TO STAY ORGANISED, MANAGE YOUR EMOTIONS, YOUR FINANCES AND SUCCEED IN LIFE

ISBN: 979-12-81498-04-4

TABLE OF CONTENTS

INTRODUCTION

ADHD can be a very difficult topic for women to discuss. Women tend to be more introverted than men, thus do not want others involved in their problems. The problem is exacerbated by society and the media that emphasize women as being family-oriented, caring, and nurturing, which makes it even harder for them to admit out loud that they have ADHD. So, how does one talk about a topic that is sensitive and often misunderstood? It is best to start off by educating yourself on the subject and then enlisting the support of significant people in your life. As you grow as a person, you should be able to handle your problems appropriately.

Attention deficit hyperactivity disorder (ADHD) is a complex brain condition that makes it hard for people to control their emotions, behaviors or focus their attention. Although ADHD affects people from all walks of life – regardless of race, religion, or socioeconomic standing – it can be particularly persistent in women. According to experts, adult women with ADHD are commonly diagnosed later than their male counterparts because they appear less disruptive and aggressive.

Most women have suffered in silence with the symptoms of their ADHD long before they are diagnosed. Women with ADHD often experience irritability, forgetfulness, and procrastination, but these symptoms are seen as normal for someone with a busy schedule. Women are estimated to have four times the prevalence of ADHD as men, but it is less likely to be diagnosed in women due to the disease's resemblance to other psychiatric disorders such as bipolar disorder or depression. On average, ADHD lasts through adolescence into adulthood, but most women do not seek help until after they have young children. Many women with ADHD remain undiagnosed until their children are older or they seek psychiatric help for other problems or injuries they have sustained.

These symptoms can make life challenging for women, especially in social situations, which can lead to isolation. For many women with ADHD, symptoms get in the way of doing basic tasks such as paying bills or making dinner. Many women are also unable to work because they lose focus while they are on the job or are tired from overworking themselves.

Because ADHD impairs a person's ability to pay attention and control their emotions, it makes it difficult for them to communicate with others and carry out daily tasks such as caring for themselves or others. As a result, many women become isolated and develop relationship issues that result in poor self-esteem and depression.

Due to the reasons above, women with ADHD are more likely than men to feel guilty, and may not speak up about their condition. This is because they do not want others to feel sorry for them or think they do not care about themselves or their families. Women with ADHD also struggle in mixed company, and social situations can be unnatural because the hyperactivity makes them want to leave and be alone. Women with ADHD can begin to feel trapped in their lives by the depression and anxiety that accompanies their symptoms, thus making it very difficult for them to deal with their disorder.

While the symptoms of adult ADHD are similar to those of childhood ADHD, women are typically diagnosed later than men because they may not be disruptive or aggressive enough for the symptoms to be noticeable. Sometimes women think that their behavior is normal and do not know that it is due to a disorder.

There are various treatments for ADHD, although many women with the condition will wait until their children are grown before seeking treatment. There is no standard protocol for treating women with ADHD, and treatment depends on the individual needs of each patient and their symptoms. Some women may benefit from medication for ADHD; however, it can be difficult for them to receive the proper diagnosis because of the similarities of ADHD with other mental disorders. This book will assist women and those who live and work with them in gaining a better understanding of the disorder and how to treat it in a healthy, safe manner.

PART 1 - UNDERSTANDING ADHD

CHAPTER 1: WHAT IS ADHD?

ADHD stands for attention deficit hyperactivity disorder. It is a mild to severe condition that affects both males and females. It is classically described in children but can persist in adulthood. ADHD affects an individual's ability to focus, stay organized, and control impulsive responses. Many adults live with untreated or undiagnosed ADHD for much of their lives.

While the exact cause of ADHD is unknown, it is thought to be caused by a combination of genetic and environmental factors. Children that suffer from ADHD are likely to have other family members who also have the disorder. It also seems that the symptoms of ADHD are triggered by certain environmental factors, though none have been isolated.

Some of the environmental factors that have been associated with ADHD are school schedules, changes in family structure, poverty, poor nutrition, and stress.

The symptoms of ADHD include disorganized behavior, inability to remain focused for extended periods, hyperactivity (excessively fidgeting or being overly active), impulsivity (acting without thinking things through), or mild to severe defiance. Many people have an understanding of these symptoms due to their understanding of children with ADHD. However, there are some other symptoms found in adults with ADHD. These include problems with daily living skills such as job performance or family relationships.

ADHD impairs the way people think, behave, and get things done. The symptoms can be different in females and males. Some women with ADHD might not have had an official diagnosis of ADHD because their symptoms don't "fit the mold" or because of a gender bias in doctors or teachers interpreting their behaviors as a "girls will be girls" type thing. Women with ADHD may have more problems at home, socializing, and managing their lives than men with ADHD. The good news is that after puberty, women are more likely to be diagnosed with attention deficit disorder, which means they are more likely to receive the necessary assistance.

WHAT CAUSES ADHD?

ADHD is a genetic disorder that affects how the brain works. It's something that's passed down by genes, so children of parents with ADHD have a greater chance of having it than the general population.

Problems with dopamine and norepinephrine levels in certain areas of the brain are thought to be the cause of ADHD. Dopamine and norepinephrine are brain chemicals that affect how information is processed and transmitted, and they're thought to be very important for attention regulation. The levels of these chemicals are affected by the amount of the hormones estrogen and testosterone.

Estrogen helps develop the brain, while testosterone affects how much dopamine, norepinephrine, and other chemicals are released in certain brain areas. Some scientists believe that for some people with ADHD, their brains don't respond optimally to either hormone.

Some researchers suspect that ADHD in girls is more likely to be caused by a combination of factors, such as genetics and environmental factors. Scientists aren't sure why the symptoms of ADHD in girls differ from those in boys, but it's possible that males' and females' brains function differently, and particularly because estrogen levels are different during puberty. It's also possible that these differences between male and female brains have nothing to do with hormones but instead have more to do with differences in how boys and girls are treated differently by society.

Genetic Factors

ADHD can run in families, so if someone close to you has ADHD, you are more likely to have it too. Studies show a 50-60% chance that someone who has ADHD in their family will also have the condition. However, only about 20% of people diagnosed with ADHD had a parent or sibling diagnosed or treated for it at some time during childhood. The chances of inheriting ADHD from your mother are 1 in 3, and the chances of inheriting it from your father are 1 in 5.

Other studies have shown that the number of people diagnosed with ADHD increases with each generation. This supports the theory that ADHD is passed down through genetics. However, it's not clear why more cases of ADHD are being treated later on in life. It could be for many reasons, including better diagnostic tools and an increased willingness on behalf of parents to get help for their children.

Environmental Factors

Many of the same factors that lead to ADHD in children also cause it in adults. These behaviors may be created by disturbances in how the brain is wired. For example, some experts believe that stressful and overwhelming situations and experiences may cause changes in metabolism and neurotransmitter levels. These differences can cause even mild ADHD issues to seem pretty serious.

These situations and experiences change how the brain communicates with other parts of the nervous system, which disrupts attention, motor control, and overall behavior, as well as neurochemical changes such as increased norepinephrine or decreased dopamine activity. Experiences such as abuse or neglect or frequent exposure to toxins like pesticides may increase your chances of developing ADHD.

ADHD is also thought to be a result of high levels of stress in the body. Studies have found that children who are constantly stressed are more likely to have ADHD, and that this link between stress and ADHD may be due to the fact that children who are stressed have less dopamine activity in their brains.

Overly permissive parenting can also lead to problems with attention.

Societal Factors

The way society treats women with ADHD could be contributing to their symptoms. For example, it's thought that girls who other kids tease for misbehaving or not doing what they're supposed to do are more likely to develop symptoms of ADHD. This may be because they feel like their behavior is unexpected or unusual, making them even more anxious and embarrassed about acting out. Hence, they resort to other behaviors such as over-eating or over-spending to try to control their emotions.

Groups of boys and girls may also be treated differently from one another. It's thought that this may lead to behavioral differences, such as more teasing and bullying in girls, which can cause anxiety-driven behaviors such as perfectionism and procrastination. Peer pressure or expectations about how to act can also affect ADHD symptoms.

Pregnancy-Related Factors

New research has shown that women who are pregnant are more likely to have ADHD. It's thought that this is because of changes in dopamine levels in pregnant women, which may affect how their brains process information.

The brain of the mother starts to change when a baby is conceived. This process is called "neurulation" and is marked by changes in dopamine levels. It's thought that pregnant women produce less dopamine, making them feel more anxious and distracted, which can cause ADHD symptoms to worsen. It's still unclear if this change happens because of pregnancy or if it's a result of the physical labor required to give birth.

In other words, pregnancy-related changes to dopamine levels may have something to do with the development of ADHD in pregnant women, but more research is needed. New moms also tend to be mentally and physically overwhelmed, which can lead to an increase in their symptoms.

ADHD affects the way our brains process information, which in turn affects how we act. The causes of ADHD are likely to be complicated and interwoven, so there's no single cause of the condition. However, experts believe that certain common factors may contribute to or trigger ADHD.

The research into male and female brains shows physical differences between the sexes that affect both male and female ADHD behaviors. Women show more attention issues, while men are more likely to have problems with behavior and moods. Anxiety is diagnosed more frequently in women than in men. Men are less likely to seek help for their disorder because of how they perceive the condition, while women are more likely to seek treatment.

The following sections discuss the roles that biology, genes, and hormones play in ADHD.

Heritability

People usually think of DNA (deoxyribonucleic acid) as a blueprint for building proteins or cells. However, DNA also contains long strands of deoxyribonucleic acid that tell our bodies when to make proteins – proteins like dopamine and norepinephrine. These proteins help brain cells communicate with each other to figure out what's going on in the body and help us keep track of things we have to do so we don't forget. These

ARE important parts of our brain! Now you know why ADHD is called a "mental disorder".

Because our DNA contains the instructions for making the proteins that help us think, act and behave, it's possible that certain genes are linked to ADHD. As discussed earlier, some believe that ADHD is directly related to genetics.

Scientists know quite a bit about how specific genes make certain proteins based on the DNA code. They have known for a long time that ADHD runs in families. Genes are part of the reason why ADHD is diagnosed more often with a first-degree family member, like a parent or sibling, than with other members of your family, like grandparents or second cousins. Parents pass their genes on to their kids and this is how ADHD occurs in families.

CHAPTER 2: EXPLORING THE HISTORICAL TIMELINE OF ADHD

Although it is relatively new to the scientific world, people have exhibited symptoms similar to ADHD throughout history. It has affected people in different centuries and countries, and its core symptoms have remained constant: inattention, hyperactivity, and impulsivity.

ADHD has been closely analyzed over the past few decades, and the medical community has come up with a more accurate diagnosis. Before this, there were no criteria for ADHD. It was just considered a behavioral disorder, making it much more difficult to diagnose. ADHD used to be known as "minimal brain damage," which is an inaccurate term when looking at modern-day knowledge of the disorder.

Some of the earliest records of ADHD come from ancient Rome, in around 400 B.C. In this era, there was a well-known problem involving students struggling in school because they could not pay attention in class. This issue would concern educators and parents alike because it affected their ability to learn and grow as students. Some scholars thought that the problem was not in the child's ability but with their behavior. Very little was known about ADHD at this point in history.

The Roman Empire was a warlike one, and many soldiers died in battles because they couldn't focus or forgot what they were supposed to be doing. The Romans did not have a word or term to describe this problem, but they did have a solution: public whipping. The government would whip the soldiers when they did not pay attention to their tasks.

In 1902, a neurologist named Dr. George Still coined the term "minimal brain damage," which is inaccurate when referring to the disorder. This paper outlined a number of criteria which is still used to diagnose children with ADHD today. Dr. Still's work helped lay the groundwork for psychological evaluations of children with attention problems at school and at home, despite some changes and additions to his work.

As time went on, the name "minimal brain damage" became outdated, and "hyperkinetic disorder" replaced it. Since ADHD does not cause brain damage, the name was changed again to attention deficit disorder (ADD). ADD is still used in some parts of the world, but in 1980 it was replaced by the current term used today: attention deficit hyperactivity disorder (ADHD).

TYPES OF ADHD

There are different types of ADHD. The main types are hyperactive, inattentive, and combined type.

Hyperactive

Those with a hyperactive type of ADHD have extremely high energy levels and tend to be more impulsive. People with this type of ADHD are the most likely to be rejected by society. They tend to make more mistakes, and have an easier time becoming distracted and losing focus.

Inattentive

Those with this type of ADHD are less active but more impulsive. They are easily distracted and tend to lose focus easily. They are more likely to grow up hating themselves because of their lack of energy. They are more prone to depression and mood swings because they cannot do what they want to do, nor can they finish what they start. Their feeling usually leads to anger or anxiety, which causes them even more frustration. They often end up hating themselves more because of the fact that they cannot do what others can do with ease or skill.

Combined-Type

Those who have the combined type of ADHD are very ener-getic, impulsive, and distracted. They also tend to lose focus easily. This is why they suffer from not finishing their tasks and make more mistakes than the other types. They often go through life feeling like a failure.

THE CORE SYMPTOMS OF ADHD

The core symptoms of ADHD are as follows:

Failing to Pay Attention

People with ADHD have trouble paying attention to what others are doing and what is going on around them. This can cause them to miss or forget details. It can affect their academic performance, and can lead to arguments with family and other people. It can also lead to people with ADHD doing things without first thinking about them and getting into trouble as a result. People with ADHD may also talk excessively, interrupt others, and blurt out answers before a question has been completed, or misplace their things frequently.

Impulsivity

Impulsivity is defined as acting on a whim without thinking about the consequences of the action. People with ADHD are often impulsive, have low self-esteem, and develop obsessive-compulsive behaviors.

Inattention

People who struggle to pay attention often have trouble concentrating on tasks, and often find it hard to finish a task, remember things, focus on details, follow directions, and report the facts of and exercise or event. This can also cause them to misplace their belongings frequently.

Inappropriate Behaviors

A person may talk excessively in a social situation without thinking of the consequences of their actions. They may also interrupt conversations, blurt out answers before questions are finished, act without thinking about the consequences of their actions, and exhibit hyperactivity.

Hyperactivity

People with ADHD often act impulsively or on a whim without thinking about the consequences beforehand. They talk excessively in social situations and may interrupt others while they are speaking. Hyperactivity can also mean that people squirm around excessively in their seats at school or in meetings at work. They may move around constantly or fidget. This can affect their ability to complete projects or tasks because they feel restless and need to move around in order to feel good.

Anxiety (Including Depression)

People with ADHD may also suffer from anxiety. Anxiety can cause people with ADHD to worry excessively about getting things done and can cause them to get easily distracted by things that bring them anxiety. This can affect their ability to focus on school or college work, and it can cause difficulty in completing tasks. It may also trigger anxiety attacks (a sudden feeling of panic, terror, or dread).

Bouts of Rage

This is when a person with ADHD has violent feelings towards the world around them. This could be because they are having a bad day, or they are overwhelmed by their symptoms. It could also be because they are being teased or tormented by someone.

Frequent Accidents

People with ADHD may also suffer frequent accidents at home or at school. This is because they are prone to losing focus on the task at hand and not paying attention to details. They may not see something in front of them or may misjudge how far away it is, which could lead to an accident.

WHAT TYPES OF BEHAVIORS DO ADULTS WITH ADHD HAVE?

Hyperactivity in Adults

This is when people feel like they need to move around in order to function. If they are in a situation where they cannot move, they may develop feelings of anxiety or panic. They may also distract themselves by making noises or fidgeting.

Impulsivity in Adults

Impulsivity can manifest itself as interrupting others when they are speaking, blurting out answers before questions have been fully asked, or finishing other people's sentences for them. People with impulsive behaviors may get into conflicts with others because of these impulsive actions.

Inattention in Adults

Adults with inattention may struggle to complete projects, have difficulty focusing on a task for long periods of time, and frequently misplace their belongings. Inattention in adults may also lead to a person changing jobs or meeting with failure in school or college because they cannot stay on task when required.

Memory Problems in Adults

People with ADHD may have trouble remembering what is going on around them, the names of people they meet, and where they put their things. They also tend to have memory lapses when it comes to dates and schedules. They may forget appointments or miss deadlines at work or school. They may often joke about their memory issues may not realize that it is causing them problems in life.

Emotional Unresponsiveness in Adults

Emotions are hard for most people with ADHD to control. They may appear insensitive to the feelings of others because they are not able to fully understand their own or other people's emotions. They may also be overly emotional and embarrass themselves by crying at the drop of a hat or becoming frustrated with seemingly insignificant things.

Impulse Buying in Adults

This is when a person with ADHD buys things without thinking of the consequences. This can lead to financial troubles that are difficult for adults with ADHD to control.

Anxiety in Adults

People with ADHD may be overly sensitive to the world around them and to their own emotions. They may interpret minor events as threatening, or they may panic easily when others are angry or frustrated with them. This can lead to anxiety attacks where a person loses all sense of reality, and their body goes numb, but worst of all, they lose the ability to think clearly and/or manage their behavior in order to prevent any harm from coming to themselves or others.

Bouts of Rage in Adults

This is when a person loses control of his or her calm and turns into a rage monster because of an upsetting situation. They might start hitting things around them or verbally attacking people. When a person with ADHD has a bout of rage, they can injure themselves or others.

Frequent Accidents in Adults

Frequent accidents in adults can cause problems at work or school, as well as problems with personal relationships.

When it comes to dealing with these issues, the first half of the puzzle is figuring out what's causing the symptoms. The other half, which is just as important, is understanding what to do when these symptoms present themselves. This is where most people with ADHD come up short.

The good news is that there is hope. ADHD can be managed and controlled very effectively if a person is willing to work at it. They can find themselves focusing on important tasks that they have long wanted to accomplish but could never manage to get done. They can feel a sense of achievement and self-worth that they had not felt for many years.

For the vast majority of children, ADHD is a condition that they outgrow and eventually control as they mature into adulthood. But for many adults, ADHD is a lifelong condition that they must learn how to manage. The key to success is a combination of identifying and testing for the right ADHD medication and attending CBT therapy sessions to learn effective coping skills for managing their ADHD symptoms.

Getting the correct diagnosis is crucial. If a person with ADHD does not have a diagnosis, they are not receiving any treatment at all. This means their symptoms will only get worse over time.

Adults are particularly susceptible to suffering from undiagnosed ADHD because the symptoms can be hard to recognize in yourself. And when people with ADHD don't receive the correct diagnosis, their issues may be incorrectly attributed to other conditions or disorders.

CHAPTER 3: IDENTIFYING ADHD SYMPTOMS IN WOMEN

Women with ADHD often suffer in silence or don't even realize they have ADHD. Symptoms can be hidden from their partners and family for a long time.

Physical Symptoms of ADHD in Women

The physical symptoms of ADHD can be especially subtle in women, but they are still present.

Women with ADHD may feel faint or get unusually lightheaded when doing simple tasks like reading or writing. They may feel like they will faint when standing for long periods or after moving quickly from sitting to standing. Women also report feeling suffocated when their chest gets tight and it becomes hard to breathe. This sensation can happen even when lying down, especially at night while trying to sleep. Tachycardia (or heart palpitations) is another physical condition that is often associated with ADHD.

Women with ADHD may also feel restless, especially in the morning. They may constantly fidget with their hands or feet or pace around the room for no reason.

Cognitive Symptoms of ADHD in Women

Women with ADHD tend to be overthinkers, making them less capable of dealing with life's pressures. They are constantly thinking about plans they will make, past events they wish they could change, or things they wish would happen. This can turn into worry, and ultimately worry can become depression if it is not addressed. Many people with ADHD constantly feel like crying.

Overthinking is just one of the many cognitive symptoms of ADHD that manifests itself in women. Problems with time management are common, as is an inability to pay attention. They may attempt to multitask, but are usually unaware that this causes them to miss steps rather than complete tasks properly. They may also have difficulty concentrating and organizing their thoughts. Many women with ADHD will admit that it feels as though time is always passing too quickly for them to do anything efficiently.

Emotional Symptoms of ADHD in Women

Stress, depression, and anxiety are also common symptoms of ADHD in women; however, these symptoms are often hidden beneath the surface. Women with ADHD may appear calm on the outside, even though deep down inside, they feel like they are failing at life no matter what they do. They are often sensitive about their problems and are at their most level-headed when talking about them. They may not understand why studying is so hard or why they always get so anxious around exams. More likely than not, they may be feeling overwhelmed and worry that if they do poorly in these situations, their parents and friends will criticize them.

Women with ADHD also tend to suffer from other mental health issues like anxiety and depression; however, these can be harder to spot because women don't always realize the link between mental health issues and their ADHD. This is especially true for women who marry or become mothers. According to one study, mothers who have ADHD (and do not take medication for it) are more distressed than either non-ADHD mothers or non-mothers with the disorder.

While there is no doubt that ADHD is associated with a variety of mental health problems, the symptoms can sometimes go undetected.

Behavioral Symptoms of ADHD in Women

While male sufferers of hyperactivity tend to act out in public, women tend to act out in private. Studies show that women with ADHD are more likely to feel bored, frustrated, and anxious when they are alone than in the company of other people. They may choose to play with their hair or fidget with their clothes or makeup. This is because they feel these behaviors release them from mental pressure.

Many women who have ADHD will engage in risky behavior to get rid of this pressure. This can be alcohol or drug abuse, gambling or making poor financial decisions. Other symptoms of ADHD can manifest themselves in negative ways later in life. Some people may become impulsive and compulsively engage in risky behavior like driving while intoxicated, smoking cigarettes, getting involved with dangerous men, etc. Another more prominent symptom is promiscuity. Seventy-one percent of women with ADHD have engaged in some kind of risky or compulsive behavior since they became adults.

People with ADHD have a unique thought process, but it does not necessarily mean they will not follow through with their plans. Many people with ADHD have a very active mind and do things that help them gain awareness about the issues that are bothering them. The problem is that their minds are so active, there's a very good chance they will forget what they were going to do next. This can lead to a lot of problems for people – especially women – with ADHD.

Most women with ADHD have many things going on in their lives at once. When they consider all of the tasks that must be completed, it may feel as though they will never be able to complete them all. Some studies estimate that women with ADHD fall short of reaching their goals 25% more often than those without ADHD.

ADHD is an issue that has been researched and studied most in males. A common misconception is that the symptoms of ADHD in women are better hidden and more likely to be overlooked when compared to symptoms in males, which can make it difficult for doctors and therapists to diagnose. This may be partly due to the fact that ADHD symptoms in females tend to manifest themselves differently than symptoms in males, who often struggle with impulsivity issues and compulsive behaviors such as binge eating or compulsive gambling. Often, women with ADHD report that they did not realize they had a problem. This can make it difficult for women to receive proper treatment.

Because ADHD is so prevalent in women, its symptoms are frequently misdiagnosed as those of other disorders. The diagnostic criteria for ADHD include difficulty staying attentive to one thing for an extended period of time, difficulty controlling behavior, and hyperactivity. These symptoms can be attributed to other disorders such as depression or anxiety disorder, so it is important for women who suspect they have ADHD to be tested by a professional.

PARENTAL CONCERNS ABOUT THE EXISTENCE OF ADHD IN

GIRLS

The idea that ADHD in women and girls is a myth seems to have been around since the 1980s. However, with a slew of scientific studies published in 2019, it's becoming more and more apparent that ADHD is simply different when it affects females.

Parents may have concerns over whether their daughter has ADHD. Research shows that ADHD in females is a real condition, but some parents still wonder whether it exists. Their doubts stem from the fact that many of the classic symptoms of ADHD, such as hyperactivity and impulsiveness, tend to be associated with male children. This makes people question whether girls can have ADHD. However, studies show that about 10% of all children diagnosed with ADHD are female.

A we have discussed, several medical conditions have similar symptoms to ADHD, so it can be difficult for people to objectively decide if a child truly has this condition or not. For example, children with ADHD also often have problems with anxiety and depression. It can be hard to tell whether ADHD is the cause of these problems or whether these conditions are because of ADHD. Furthermore, children may have trouble paying attention due to a physical ailment, such as hearing loss or vision impairment.

Scientists and doctors who work in the area of ADHD in females are well aware of these concerns. A recent study examined girls who were referred to clinics for auditory processing issues. These girls had no other symptoms of ADHD; they all passed hearing tests and had an IQ that did not fall below 85 points. The researchers suspected that this group of children had ADHD, but they also wanted to ensure that the girls did not suffer from a different cognitive problem. They decided to compare the girls with other children with ADHD who did have other symptoms.

These results are useful because they show that a girl can have none of the classic ADHD symptoms and still be diagnosed with the disorder by medical professionals. Over 30% of these girls were previously diagnosed with another cognitive ailment, such as hearing loss or reticence to speak.

It's important to remember that ADHD is a condition that often masquerades as other cognitive ailments. This is why a doctor or psychologist needs to administer comprehensive tests to diagnose this condition accurately.

THE DIFFERENCES BETWEEN ATTENTION-DEFOCUSED AND ATTENTION-DIVERTED SUBTYPES OF ADHD

Research shows that there are, in fact, fundamental differences between how attention-focused and attention-diverted women experience ADHD.

Attention-focused women are more likely to be hyper-focused on goals and tasks, which can benefit their careers. However, these goals can change every day or even every hour, depending on the project or task at hand. They may feel less able to switch gears when faced with a new task or assignment than those without ADHD. This intense focus often leaves them exhausted but fulfilled at the end of the day. And while they may have trouble "switching gears" quickly, they are better at sustaining their attention to one topic for longer periods than those with other forms of ADHD.

Attention-diverted women struggle with achieving goals, as well as creating and maintaining good habits. These are the classic symptoms of ADHD, which can be extremely disruptive to their day-to-day lives. They may find it difficult to maintain lifestyle changes as adults. They may have trouble finishing tasks or simply procrastinate each night after work.

The good news is that both attention-focused and attention-diverted women can overcome their ADHD symptoms, heal their relationship with it, and use it to their advantage. Many of the symptoms can be managed or even eliminated through the use of brain training techniques and medications. For both attention-focused and attention-diverted women, these improvements are vital for progression in life and a sense of fulfillment. They can learn how to control their emotions, set boundaries, work with a coach or therapist, effectively manage situation stressors, rely more on their strengths, and become more self-sufficient.

CHAPTER 4:
THE DIFFICULTY
OF DIAGNOSING
ADHD IN WOMEN

Women are often expected to be "shiny happy people." If they show any signs of being "out of control," they are viewed as overly emotional. Women with ADHD may struggle to get the proper diagnosis or treatment, for reasons discussed in the previous chapter. This is a common challenge for many women with ADHD.

Because they believe society looks down on them because they aren't "shining," women with ADHD are less likely to seek help or treatment. They may have difficulty living up to the expectations of others about how a woman should act.

As a result of this shame, many women do not feel comfortable discussing their issues with their family or friends. They do not confide in the people they love because they don't want them to judge them. A woman's relationships may be filled with drama as a result of her ADHD.

This shame can also cause women with ADHD to live their lives in two worlds. The public face of the social mask hides their struggles, and the private face shows their true selves. They can detach from themselves by mentally going off into another world, losing themselves in daydreams or even in alcohol or other drugs. Some women report having severe problems with dissociation as a result of this detachment.

There are a variety of reasons why diagnosing ADHD in women is difficult, some of which are related to gender differences. Several of the most prevalent are as follows:

Variability

Women often show signs of ADHD across different settings. They may show symptoms in public but appear to have it together at home, or vice versa. Even if they appear to follow a routine, there is likely variability in their lives that they don't see because they are trying to hold everything together. This can result in different behaviors depending on the situation.

Shyness

Women can be more naturally introverted and shy than men. The symptoms of ADHD can make them feel uncomfortable in social settings, so they avoid or leave interactions early. Additionally, women with ADHD were often teased or verbally abused as children. They may have learned to use their "mask" to protect themselves from others' negative comments about their behavior. This introversion may cause them to appear depressed or even anxious, which can lead people to think that these women have more severe problems than just ADHD.

Attention to Detail

Women are often more detail-oriented than men. They can be especially sensitive to things as small as when others cross their line of sight or when they are overheard by someone else. Consequently, they may be more likely to notice details other people may not even notice, which can be a significant factor in their feeling out of control. This trait can cause women to overanalyze situations or give them the impression that other people are unkind or insensitive when the opposite is happening in reality. Attention to detail leads some people with ADHD to obsess over small details, which can also cause them anxiety. They may spend all day on one thing that is not important and lose track of time without realizing it.

Planning and Organization Difficulties

Women are usually more concerned with the future than men. They may have difficulties with tasks that require planning, organization, and time management. Women's ADHD often manifests itself as a lack of organization or planning skills, and consequently, they feel that things around them are out of control or heading in the wrong direction.

Overthinking

Women are usually more concerned with other people's opinions about them, particularly if those opinions are negative. They will obsess over how the world perceives them and whether the "right" things are being said about them. This can be very stressful because it can lead to a host of other issues such as depression and anxiety. They may become obsessed with how others perceive their thoughts and actions. This is especially problematic for women with ADHD because they can't control what other people think about them, so they might spend a lot of time worrying about it! It may cause a woman to have difficulty making decisions or prioritizing tasks because she can't concentrate on one thing at a time. This can be difficult to live with because it takes a lot of energy and may cause addictions or substance abuse.

Difficult Childhood Experiences

Many women who have ADHD experienced childhood trauma, abuse, or neglect in some form. The struggle to cope with these experiences can cause them to feel like they cannot do anything right. This can also manifest itself in other ways, such as depression and anxiety, which may be misdiagnosed as ADHD.

These childhood experiences can cause a lot of pain and anguish that is difficult to deal with later in life. They may even have difficulty accepting their ADHD for cognitive reasons. This can lead to confusion and frustration for the people around them and can cause them to feel unloved, abandoned, or confused.

Behavioral Problems in Adult Life

Many women who struggle with ADHD have been through some trauma in their lives. Whether physical, sexual, or emotional abuse, it can be difficult for them to deal with their behavior as they try to adjust back into society. It is also common for women with ADHD to struggle with substance abuse or self-harm as they try desperately to cope with feelings that they may not understand themselves. If you are struggling with these issues, don't be bashful. Get help. There are a lot of professionals who will be able to help you improve your quality of life and get back to the person you used to be. You're not alone, and it's not your fault.

Over-responsibility, or "Greater Good Syndrome"

Women with ADHD may feel obligated to look after everyone else and make sure that everything in their lives runs smoothly. They may feel a strong sense of responsibility for those around them, believing that it is expected of them as the "better half." They may also believe they are owed something for their life's sacrifices due to the amount of work they put in. Because people often have a hard time asking for help in the first place, this can cause a lot of stress and anxiety. Women with ADHD may feel guilty and responsible for what they perceive to be the negative actions of others. They may also feel responsible for all the negative things that happen in their lives, even when they have no control over them.

Many women struggle with ADHD, but it is important to recognize that you do not need to be defined by your condition, and that there are many ways in which the condition can be managed and treated.

CHAPTER 5: THE BIOLOGICAL BASIS OF ADHD IN WOMEN

A DHD affects multiple systems in the brain and body. The neuroendocrine system, neurotransmitters, the autonomic nervous system (ANS), and the central nervous system are among them (CNS).

Neuroendocrine System

The neuroendocrine system is a complex hormonal network involved with many of our bodily functions like cognitive development and memory function. It is also responsible for regulating stress response and coping abilities, particularly those concerned with emotion regulation. Neuroendocrine system imbalances are more common in women with ADHD than in men with ADHD. This may manifest as a delayed onset of puberty, irregular menses, and an underactive sex drive.

Neurotransmitters

Neurotransmitters are the chemicals that allow communication across the synapses in our brains. They act as chemical messengers between nerve cells to facilitate information transmission. When this system is working well, we learn and remembering new things relatively easily. When it does not work well, our ability to learn and remember new things can be impaired greatly. Slower cognitive function and memory problems may result. Women with ADHD have been shown to have less neurotransmitter dopamine in their brains than men with ADHD. This is important because dopamine is responsible for the reward pathway in the brain. When we experience pleasure, our body releases dopamine into this pathway which motivates us to repeat 'pleasurable' actions. The pleasure associated with these actions reinforces behavior (learning) that we consider pleasurable or rewarding. Dopamine also is involved with motivation, attention, and learning.

Autonomic Nervous System

The ANS is the part of our nervous system that regulates and controls bodily functions like heart rate, digestion, body temperature, and perspiration. It is divided into the sympathetic part (activated in times of stress) and the parasympathetic part (activated in relaxation). Women with ADHD tend to have lower activity in their parasympathetic nervous system. This may result in hyperactivity, as well as problems with focusing and filtering aggression out of emotions. The fight or flight response, which allows us to respond appropriately when danger is perceived, is a part of the ANS, and its effects on the body include increased heart rate, dilated pupils, increased respiration, and increased blood flow to skeletal muscle. If a person is not able to react appropriately because their parasympathetic nervous system does not function properly, these tasks may not be accomplished as effectively or quickly, resulting in anxiety, fearfulness, and sudden outbursts of anger.

Central Nervous System

The CNS is responsible for regulating all the other systems in the body. It allows us to feel pleasure and pain through our neurons, spinal cord, and peripheral nervous system. The CNS is also responsible for the movement and coordination of the body. Because women with ADHD tend to have less dopamine in their brains, they often struggle with getting enough motivation to perform a task, making them very vulnerable to addictive behaviors like substance abuse. Women with ADHD also tend to exhibit low levels of myelin in their brains, resulting in slower transmission of information between neurons. This leads to a decreased ability to think quickly, control impulsive behavior, and organize thoughts effectively.

Inattention, which presents as a constant habit of distraction and lack of focus, is the most common symptom for women with ADHD. This could be because women are more adept at multitasking than men. Inattention has a biological basis as well. Because they have lower levels of dopamine in their brains, which is responsible for paying attention and focusing on the tasks at hand, women with ADHD are more easily distracted in everyday life than men with ADHD. Women with ADHD are also more prone to forgetfulness, procrastination, and losing track of time.

The hyperactivity in women with ADHD is explained by the fact that their bodies tend to produce greater amounts of adrenaline than those without ADHD. Adrenaline allows people to 'hyper-focus' or concentrate intently on a particular task or subject for a period of time. However, when this focus is over, people with ADHD tend to feel restless, agitated, fidgety, and fatigued. They may seek out excitement and thrills because their bodies are so tired but stimulated by adrenaline. This is why women with ADHD tend to be highly impulsive and have a hard time focusing. They are also more vulnerable to addictive or compulsive behaviors because of the way their brain responds to dopamine.

Women with ADHD have a hard time focusing on multiple tasks at once and often have trouble organizing themselves for long periods of time. Moreover, women with ADHD tend to be more impulsive, which can affect their memory.

Many women with ADHD have reading, writing, and/or math disabilities but are able to "mask" their ADHD symptoms when they are in an environment that is conducive to their learning style. When these women reach adulthood, however, they find it much more difficult to cope with their condition because the high levels of stress and expectations associated with the adult world are not as easily compensated for by the ADHD brain.

Another symptom of the disorder is emotional liability, which encompasses both overreacting or underreacting emotionally under different circumstances. Women who suffer from this symptom may become very upset when they do not receive enough praise from others. As a result, they may not obtain the positive feedback they desire and consequently develop feelings of inadequacy, depression, or anxiety.

PART 2 - THE EFFECTS OF ADHD

CHAPTER 6: A DISTRACTED MIND

It's not just everyday activities that can be affected by ADHD. Women with ADHD often feel especially overwhelmed in social situations. They may find it difficult to focus on what's being said, track the conversation, remember what people are talking about, or keep up with the high-speed give and take of family gatherings or work meetings. While their minds may be racing, they often struggle to make eye contact, listen directly, and stay engaged. As a result, they may be viewed as aloof or not paying attention.

The Attention Deficit Disorder Association says that women with ADHD "may be prone to misreading social cues and responding inappropriately in social situations. They might also have a tendency toward negative self-talk and passivity, which can make them less assertive than they need to be in their social lives."

The Challenges of Multitasking

Maintaining attention and prioritizing while juggling multiple tasks is one of the biggest challenges for women with ADHD. They may have trouble determining which task should be tackled first, what to do if they're interrupted, and how interruptions will affect the overall timeline. While multitasking can seem like a good solution in some situations, it's often a recipe for frustration and loss of productivity.

Making the Most of Time and Space

Women with ADHD may have a hard time managing their time, especially when they are rushing to complete tasks. They may feel overwhelmed by nonessential tasks and forget to do what matters. They also tend to get stuck in a negative cycle of "do-nothing" syndrome. This can be problematic if bad procrastination, poor planning, and unproductive working patterns block their progress.

Women with ADHD may need to create a routine that includes clear expectations, consistent follow-through, or the use of external motivators to help them get the job done. Regular check-ins with their boss can also be helpful.

A DISTRACTED LIFE

ADHD is often a symptom of underlying conditions like depression, anxiety, or trauma. When it occurs on its own, it can be a source of extra stress and can make life even more challenging. Many women with ADHD may have difficulty adjusting to different (or changing) locations and environments. They may also find it difficult to make new friends or feel lonely. This can lead to depression, which is one of the most common comorbidities in women with ADHD.

Academic problems are also common among women with ADHD who struggle to focus on schoolwork, often because their brains are overstimulated. When they can't make it to class, they may feel like they are failing. They may also question their intelligence, a self-fulfilling prophecy that creates more anxiety and depression. However, learning disabilities (such as dyslexia), sensory processing problems (such as tactile defensiveness or tactile processing disorder), and other conditions that cause inattention can also be misinterpreted as ADHD.

Staying Healthy

Women with ADHD often have a hard time making healthy food choices, or they may be so busy that they forget to eat. The consequences may include weight gain, low energy levels, and trouble sleeping. Sleep problems are also common among women with ADHD, especially if they take stimulant medications or have co-existing conditions like insomnia or restless leg syndrome.

Stress is the enemy of wellness and can cause a number of physical and emotional problems. Some women with ADHD have difficulty dealing with stressful situations, leading to anxiety, poor coping skills, anger, and depression.

Low-level chronic stress (common among people with ADHD) can cause the body to produce extra cortisol, the primary stress hormone, according to a 2014 study published by the National Institute of Health. Over time, this can lead to higher C-reactive protein levels (CRP), a marker for inflammation and cardiovascular disease. "This means that people with ADHD may be at increased risk for developing atherosclerosis, even though they're young," says Michael Rucklidge, MD, a professor of psychiatry at the University of Hawaii at Manoa, and lead author of the study.

The Impact on Relationships

The symptoms of ADHD can create significant challenges in a relationship, whether it's between a parent and child, between partners in a romantic relationship, or among members of the same family. Women with ADHD may have difficulty paying attention, listening, remembering details, and managing anger. A partner may notice that they are easily distracted or short-tempered. They might have trouble connecting with children, keeping up with household chores, or helping with homework.

Many women with ADHD have difficulty managing their feelings and controlling their behavior in a relationship. They may display mood swings, become verbally abusive or passive-aggressive, and feel they can't trust their partners. Relationship problems can cause tension and create frustration for both partners, increasing the risk of violence and divorce.

Studies show that women who have ADHD are more likely to report abusive partners. If a woman wants to get help for her ADHD, she may need to consider putting a safety plan in place first.

Social Life, Education, and Work

Women with ADHD may have a hard time fitting in socially, managing their emotions, or making decisions. They may have difficulty finding the right friends, often struggling to relate to people of diverse personalities and life experiences. This can also be a problem when they are trying to build or maintain a professional network.

Women who suffer from ADHD may find it difficult to concentrate on schoolwork, complete projects, and assignments, and follow directions, all of which can lead to academic difficulties. They may also tend toward disorganization and procrastination that can make schoolwork even more difficult to manage. However, some women with ADHD are hyper-focused on certain things and manage to do very well in school.

Job-seeking can be especially challenging for women with ADHD, who may find it hard to manage emotions, remain focused during interviews, or follow through with scheduled meetings. To achieve success in the workplace and advance their careers, they may need extra time to study, complete assignments or projects, and seek accommodations such as extra time on tests or a quiet place to work.

ADHD and the Law

Women with ADHD may have trouble controlling their emotions, especially when they feel their rights are being violated or treated unfairly. They may get into trouble at school, at work, in public, or with law enforcement. Although women with ADHD make up only 2-3% of prison populations, those who do commit crimes tend to be more impulsive and violent. They may become more reckless and dangerous when they can't control their behavior or feel frustrated by a lack of consequences or accountability. As an result, they have a higher chance of being arrested.

Women with ADHD may also have trouble getting their anger under control. If they are frustrated by the lack of consequences or accountability, they may get into trouble when they're angry, leading to jail time. Women with ADHD are also more likely to use illegal drugs and risk the associated health consequences.

As discussed earlier, women with ADHD are more likely to end up in an abusive relationship. Most states have certain laws that protect people from domestic violence and bodily harm by intentional negligence. Women in an abusive relationship may need legal action to protect themselves from dangerous situations or recover from injuries.

Domestic violence rules are complex, but women can get help working through their frustrations and obtaining legal protection. Women with ADHD have the same rights as their peers when it comes to abuse at home, but they may have problems getting access to domestic violence shelters, restraining orders, and support programs.

Many people with ADHD also experience symptoms of other mental health disorders. In rare cases, these symptoms can make it hard for others to understand what is going on in their lives or become triggering issues that lead to trouble at school or work. Women with ADHD may find that others are disconnected from them or are unable to understand what they're going through. They may feel lonely and alone, even if they have a family and friends who care about them.

Women who struggle with ADHD in a relationship may feel misunderstood and unfairly blamed. They may suffer in silence because the people around them don't appreciate the challenges they face on a day-to-day basis.

A DISTRACTED HOME

Women with ADHD are more likely to initiate divorce compared to women without ADHD, and this tends to be the case early in their marriage and after children enter the picture. Women with ADHD may experience more marital conflict over trivial things than their male counterparts and often feel disconnected from their husbands and the family as a whole.

Problems with paperwork and household tasks are one of the most common sources of marital conflict for women with ADHD. While these problems are very surface-level, they can lead to deeper issues within the marriage. Women with ADHD may be more sensitive to their husbands' moods, prone to anger outbursts, and chronically complain about their housework. These complaints can create tension between the couple, which can lead to arguments.

Problems with organizations can cause further frustration for women with ADHD and their spouses. Women with ADHD experience more difficulty in remembering things, such as when to do laundry or what is stored in which cupboard. The couple's frustration with each other spreads and begins to affect other aspects of the marriage.

Women with ADHD may have a higher infidelity rate than men with ADHD because they desire more novelty in their daily lives. Women with ADHD are three times more likely to have an extramarital affair than men with ADHD. This is sometimes brought on by sexual boredom within their marriage or the desire to feel connected to someone who understands them. Some women with ADHD, however, will not cheat on their husbands but will instead fantasize about it or even speak to that effect when they experience rejection from their spouse. When this happens, it often leads to low self-esteem and increased irritation for both parties in a relationship.

Decisions about property division and spousal support are issues that can be particularly problematic for women with ADHD who decide to divorce their spouses. These issues are amplified when the wife is inattentive and impulsive and may forget things or have poor travel plans.

When discussing property division, women approaching divorce may have difficulty understanding how they will be able to pay for housing on their own. Sometimes this comes from the assumption that they will always receive spousal support from their husbands. The same is true when it comes to cars. A woman with ADHD may assume that she can use spousal support in order to purchase a new car. Women with ADHD may also have difficulty understanding the value of their household goods, which can cause frustration for their spouses during the property division process.

Women with ADHD often feel guilt around the divorce process because they are breaking up their families, making them more prone to depression and anxiety. There is also the worry that a new partner will reject or abuse them because of their ADHD. Women with ADHD often feel overwhelmed by these emotions and fall into isolation. They can become so depressed that they do not want to leave the house.

Women with ADHD are more likely to enter a support group after they exit their marriage than men with ADHD. Women tend to need more help and support during the divorce process because of their emotions and anxiety about losing their home. However, there are also some similarities between the way men and women with ADHD use support groups. Both genders tend to have a hard time coping with their ADHD on their own and rely on positive reinforcement through these groups in order to stay motivated. There are also some differences among the genders. Men are more likely than women to only discuss their ADHD during meetings. Women with ADHD, on the other hand, utilize support groups as a place where they can talk about the divorce and seek advice, as well as social interaction.

There are several reasons why women file for divorce more than men do. Women with ADHD tend to have a higher rate of infidelity than men with ADHD and therefore can use this as a reason for their divorce. Also, women who are in violent or abusive relationships will often seek help from organizations that aid women in abusive relationships. These organizations will often give these women the confidence they need to leave the relationship and find a new one, so many women with ADHD become estranged from their husbands after entering these programs.

The social stigma against women with ADHD can really affect the way they are viewed in society. Many people will see a woman with ADHD as incapable of taking care of herself and her children, which may result in a lack of support for her through a divorce. Women with ADHD need to remember that divorce can be incredibly detrimental to their well-being.

The relationship between ADHD and divorce is well documented, but there are many options for coping with addictions and attention disorders. Marriage counseling may help resolve some of these issues before they interfere too much with your daily life. A qualified therapist can also help you learn to control your behavior.

Finally, women with ADHD often have significant challenges in education. This can create major obstacles in their career advancement and they may lose out on financial opportunities. Women with ADHD also have more difficulty getting into graduate school or obtaining comparable jobs after receiving their bachelor's degrees.

For women diagnosed with ADHD, it is important for them to talk about this issue as early as possible.

A DISTRACTED FUTURE

There is no doubt that more and more people are experiencing ADD/ADHD as we speak. In fact, in the United States, ADD/ADHD affects 3.5% of the population, with 1 in every 10 children diagnosed before age 18.

This has led to many changes and challenges for women with ADHD. In today's society, women often find it hard to balance their careers and personal lives. These women spend their days at work or school feeling like they can't quite get their work done on time, and it's not uncommon for them to feel discouraged.

LONG-TERM IMPACTS OF ADHD ON WOMEN

This issue is so prevalent that the *Journal of Attention Disorders* has a section dedicated to women and attention deficit disorders. The problems add up for women who have ADHD; it's common for them to receive less career advancement than their co-workers, and they are often held back in their careers.

Women with ADHD are also more likely to have their children diagnosed with the disorder, so it's very important for them to set up a schedule that works for them and follow through on it. Sadly, women are less likely than men to receive appropriate ADHD treatment, and as a result, they are more likely to experience medical consequences.

In conclusion, women with ADHD are not only faced with being left behind when they take on a career. Low self-esteem and self-confidence are also common issues for them. Women with ADHD are often in denial of their own problems because they have been taught that they are simply weak or undisciplined, rather than facing a disorder. Women often learn to put others before themselves, and that keeps them from overcoming their challenges. Anxiety and depression often plague women with ADHD, which can make things even more difficult.

WOMEN WITH ADHD IN THE WORKPLACE

Women often find that they are more reluctant than men to take on new jobs or jobs that require organization. They do not typically feel as enthusiastic about professional success as men do.

While it is true that women may lack the desire to work hard and get ahead, they deserve to have equal opportunities and accommodations provided by employers. A woman with ADHD who has been able to be productive and make a name for herself has completed an important step forward in her lifecycle; one that should be celebrated and acknowledged.

ADHD is considered a disorder of executive functions, which include working memory, emotional control, the ability to plan and prioritize, the ability to see the "big picture," and to think flexibly. There are three other aspects of executive function that are often related to ADHD: an over-responsibility for details, an intense interest in topics that may be trivial or obscure, and anxiety about mistakes.

Women with ADHD often have more trouble than men in executive functioning areas such as organization and planning, though these functions relate less strongly to overall success at work. In addition, women are much more likely than men to have difficulty with project numbers and details. Women with ADHD also tend to be significantly less confident about their abilities at work, so these challenges can exacerbate the problem.

As the number of women in the American workforce has increased, research on the particular issues of women with ADHD has been gaining more attention. One such study found that executive function explains about 40% of the difference between women and men in occupational attainment.

Women with ADHD are more likely to work in fields that require more physical activity and are less regimented, such as health care or education, than men are. They are also more likely than men to be distracted by their physical surroundings. For example, they may respond differently to sounds when they are at work or school compared to when they are relaxing or talking with friends or family members.

CHAPTER 7: THE DISCRIMINATION AGAINST WOMEN EXPERIENCING ADHD

S tereotype threat is a general worry that the expectations surrounding a person's identity, such as their gender, race, ethnicity, or sexual orientation, will affect their performance. Stereotype threat can be particularly challenging for women with ADHD and can make it harder to feel confident in themselves. Stereotypes of women with ADHD can make them insecure about themselves and feel less competent. Stereotype threat persists in multiple contexts, such as the classroom, work, and even among friends.

Although stereotype threat has been shown to affect women's performance in math classes negatively, it is important to recognize that it will not have an impact on all people with ADHD and may have different effects depending on the person's experience and skill level. Nonetheless, individuals need to be aware of how stereotypes affect them and how they can manage them when they appear.

Stereotype threats can occur in a wide range of situations. Stereotypes are strong negative beliefs about a particular group of people and are often based on low self-esteem and perceptions of incompetence. Any negative information about a person's identity may lead to stereotype threats. A great example of this is the stereotypical belief that women are not good at math or science. This can lead to anxiety for women with ADHD in high school and can trigger stereotypical thoughts that cause them to perform worse than they would without the anxiety.

When the presence of a stereotype or a negative belief about a person's identity impairs their performance in a situation or competition, this is referred to as a stereotype threat. As previously mentioned, this can occur in many different contexts and situations, such as in school, the workplace, and social relationships. For women with ADHD, stereotype threat can be especially problematic as this group of people is stereotyped negatively due to their low self-esteem and intelligence, leading to anxiety that results in poorer performance.

According to an article conducted by Timothy B. Smith, "stereotype threat has a negative impact on women's performance in math classes when these students are exposed to the stereotype of being poor math students."

Stereotype threat can be extremely problematic for women with ADHD and other groups who experience low self-esteem. When we deal with social interactions, we often rely on how those around us view us, so when we learn that another person does not view us positively, it may impact our interactions and our ability to feel confident in ourselves. Many studies have demonstrated the powerful effects of stereotype threat on women with ADHD and how it can negatively impact their cognitive processing abilities and performance in social situations.

Reactive attachment theory suggests that individuals with ADHD are more likely to develop avoidant and insecure attachment styles, which are associated with low self-esteem, internalization of beliefs about self and others, mistrust of others, and higher deficits in cognitive control. This makes it harder for women with ADHD to feel confident in themselves, resulting in lower confidence and feelings of incompetence.

Women with ADHD in their childbearing years may also feel negatively judged by others because of the social stigma toward ADHD and its treatment. Because they are dealing with an illness that many people don't understand or support, it can affect their self-esteem and make them feel even more insecure.

This can make it more difficult for them to parent on their own, and it may cause them to overlook important aspects of their children's emotional, physical, and intellectual development.

Stereotype threat is more damaging in women with ADHD than in men with ADHD as women are generally stereotyped as being less intelligent, leading to lower performance in various areas of life. For women who are faced with stereotype threats and do not have the coping skills to prevent it from affecting their performance, this can affect career and college path-finding decisions as well as their ability to find love.

Stereotype threat affects all women with ADHD differently. Some women may experience more anxiety than others, which can cause them to perform worse than they would without the anxiety. In areas where women's gender is given more attention than men's, stereotyping is more likely to occur. Stereotype threat affects performance in all groups of people but is made more problematic for women with ADHD due to the lack of resources available to help them.

Stereotype threat is a result of the intersectionality of gender and mental illness. Not only are women with ADHD more likely to be affected by stereotype threats, but it is also more damaging due to the social stigma around mental illness and its treatments. Stereotype threat is especially problematic in light of the stigma associated with ADHD because many people do not understand or support it. This negative perception of women, as well as people with ADHD in general, can cause them to feel inferior and unable to succeed. Because of this, stereotype threat can cause women with ADHD to feel anxiety about their ability in various situations, which may negatively affect their performance.

CHAPTER 8: ADHD AND CONCOMITANT DIAGNOSES

The symptoms of ADHD can be quite varied. ADHD frequently occurs in conjunction with other disorders. Men are more likely to have antisocial or narcissistic personality disorders, whereas women are more likely to have anxiety, depression, bipolar disorder (manic episodes), or borderline personality disorder.

Women are also more likely to experience significantly more social impairment than males because of difficulty in social cognition – understanding how others communicate via nonverbal cues. This is due to the fact that females with ADHD are more likely to have Asperger's Syndrome, obsessive-compulsive (OCD) disorder, or be diagnosed with attention-deficit/hyperactivity disorder (ADHD) combined subtype.

On the other hand, adult males are more likely than women to have antisocial personality disorder. Those who abuse alcohol or drugs may also be diagnosed with substance dependence syndrome or substance abuse syndrome.

The main symptoms of ADHD are inattention, hyperactivity, and impulsivity, but people with comorbid disorders also experience anxiety, depression, and anger. Women with ADHD often complain of oversensitivity to sound or light, a condition called sensory integration disorder. Getting diagnosed with a condition like OCD can be confusing if the individual is already diagnosed with ADHD; patients may be diagnosed with both conditions. Diagnosing those exposed to violence, trauma, or stress – especially in childhood – can sometimes be difficult because symptoms of ADHD overlap with PTSD and other conditions. Any co-occurring disorders should be diagnosed and treated before treatment for ADHD begins.

Most women with ADHD are very good at masking their symptoms and living a normal life. Because of the negative stigma related to mental health issues, many women are hesitant to admit they have a problem and seek professional help. The fear of being "labeled" exacerbates the problem. Women may wish to conceal their disorder for a variety of reasons:

- They may not know how to express their thoughts, feelings, and behaviors in a way that others can understand.

- It may be embarrassing or humiliating.

- They may feel inferior or incompetent as a result of their disorder.

- Women with ADHD may also feel uncomfortable expressing anger because they fear it will be interpreted as hostility or resentfulness.

All of the above reasons contribute to a lack of treatment for women with ADHD. To get help, a woman must first realize that her ability to function is not adequate and that she needs help. Once the patient recognizes she has a problem, they can seek out a professional who can provide an assessment to describe their thoughts, feelings, and behaviors. The diagnosis process takes time; it is an extensive effort in which professionals use both clinical interviews and psychological testing. After treatment begins, patients may have sessions with their diagnosing therapist and psychologist; this ensures continuity of care between doctors to obtain the best results possible.

Women with ADHD who have children have a high chance of their children also having the disorder. If the woman can control her symptoms, she can help her child also learn how to regulate their attention, behavior, and emotions.

When a woman becomes pregnant, the feedback system in her brain is turned on, and she needs to pay attention to all of the changes in the body. If a woman does not take adequate care of herself during pregnancy, she may feel overwhelmed, which often results in a poor diet, excessive weight gain, or even obesity. If a woman with ADHD improves her diet and exercise routine during pregnancy, she can help ensure that she has the best possible results after giving birth to her new baby.

With the proper treatment and support, women can overcome their symptoms and take advantage of the richness that comes from living an active and successful life.

COMORBIDITIES

Many women with ADHD are often misdiagnosed. The most common comorbid condition is anxiety, which is why women seek treatment for mental health disorders when in actuality, they have ADHD. In addition, women are less likely to be treated for these disorders and may not receive medication or therapy unless they present with a different condition.

The following is a list of frequently diagnosed comorbid conditions:

Anxiety

When people diagnosed with ADHD are also diagnosed with anxiety, only a small percentage of them receive treatment for ADHD. This can be because the symptoms are often similar to those of anxiety. A woman with ADHD needs to realize that if her anxiety symptoms interfere with her life, she should seek treatment.

Depression

Depression is often misdiagnosed as "normal" moodiness, which prevents women with ADHD from seeking treatment. Women with ADHD who are depressed may not recognize the signs of depression or realize that the moodiness is more than just "the blues." They may also believe that their inability to cope is a part of having ADHD rather than a separate disorder.

Substance Abuse

Women with ADHD have higher rates of substance abuse, but it is often difficult for women to admit that they have an issue with alcohol and drugs. Women with ADHD may also believe they have a problem with substance abuse rather than ADHD when there is a problem with attention, weight, or another similar symptom.

Sleep Issues

Sleeping through the night can be very difficult for women who have ADHD, and they often take naps during the day. Women who struggle with insomnia often think that if they keep going to bed at the same time each night, the problems will go away, however this is not always the case.

Dopamine Deficiency

People with ADHD are more likely to develop Parkinson's disease; they are also much more prone to developing Alzheimer's disease and have lower dopamine levels than healthy people.

Fibromyalgia

Fibromyalgia is an illness with many symptoms, but pain sensitivity is the most common. Women with ADHD are more likely to suffer from fibromyalgia than men with ADHD or those without an ADHD diagnosis.

Hallucinations

Women with ADHD who have hallucinations are more likely to be prescribed stimulant medication to treat this symptom. The medications may cause a rebound effect in which the hallucinations worsen.

Obsessive-Compulsive Disorder

Obsessive-compulsive disorder is often misdiagnosed as ADHD; this can prevent people with the two conditions from receiving proper care.

Post-Traumatic Stress Disorder

PTSD, or post-traumatic stress disorder, can be a reaction to a disturbing event experienced in a past life that has continued into adulthood. Women with PTSD are more likely than women without the disorder to be diagnosed with ADHD.

Social Phobia

One of the most common phobias, social phobia, can cause extreme avoidance in a person's life. Women with social phobias are more likely to be diagnosed with ADHD.

Tourette's Syndrome

Tourette's Syndrome causes people to make sudden, repetitive movements or sounds. It is a genetic disorder that is found in approximately 1% of school-aged children. In many cases, people with Tourette's Syndrome will show symptoms between the ages of five to fifteen. ADHD is often misdiagnosed as Tourette's Syndrome because they are similar disorders.

Tics

Tics are sudden, repetitive movements or vocalizations that people make involuntarily. Tics can be treated with medication and cognitive-behavioral therapy. Tics are often misdiagnosed as ADHD because they share many of the same symptoms.

SELF-AWARENESS AND SELF-MANAGEMENT

Many people are unaware of the link between ADHD and self-awareness. When you understand your condition better, you can become your own best advocate.

For women with ADHD, self-awareness is one of the most important concepts; knowing what to do in any situation can be difficult. Women who recognize these challenges and work through them successfully feel empowered and prepared for whatever they may face in life. They find that they are happier when they know what to do in all situations, good or bad.

For women with ADHD, self-awareness and self-management are essential to feeling happy and successful in life. No two days are identical, so women with ADHD will always be learning how to manage their lives successfully. By developing this skill early on, they find that life is easier and more fulfilling as they get older.

Let's first discuss the concept of self-awareness. Self-awareness is a person's ability to see themselves and their strengths and weaknesses. It leads to recognition, acceptance, and growth. The more a person understands themself, the more in control they feel. Having awareness and understanding how your ADHD impacts your life are two of the most important keys for successful management of the condition.

Self-awareness can also lead to happiness because you can take control of your life once you have self-awareness. If you do not know what to do or how people will react when you make decisions, you will likely feel unhappy or unable to achieve your goals.

Self-awareness can make you feel better about yourself and improve your self-esteem. It can also help you understand the world around you and can connect you to a greater sense of purpose.

Self-management refers to managing one's life constructively through reflecting on goals and values, being flexible, and having a sense of humor when things do not go as planned. This can be especially challenging for women with ADHD because they might have the best of intentions but struggle with discipline or organization. However, this is normal and should not be used as an excuse to avoid developing self-management skills.

Women who struggle with self-management might have trouble handling daily tasks and may delay important choices that could affect their lives. By being aware of these challenges, one can learn the skills of daily self-management. This can lead to healthy choices, more efficiency, and improved quality of life.

Self-management is also a key to success because it gives people the tools they need to live life on their own terms. It allows women with ADHD to be independent and self-reliant throughout the course of their lives. Being able to organize tasks, set goals, overcome challenges and frustrations, remain flexible, and maintain a positive outlook will help them have a more fulfilling life.

It's important for women with ADHD to learn how to manage their time because time management is essential for many life skills. Being able to use time wisely will help people feel more successful in life. It can also improve relationships by ensuring things get done in a timely manner, which makes people feel like you respect them or want to help them.

PART 3
- DISCOVERING WAYS TO SEEK ASSISTANCE FOR WOMEN WITH ADHD

CHAPTER 9: GETTING AN ACCURATE DIAGNOSIS

Getting the right diagnosis for ADHD is paramount. Getting the wrong diagnosis can be more harmful than helpful and can lead to a life of feeling misunderstood, unvalued, and under-appreciated. When seeking a diagnosis, it is important to choose a psychiatrist experienced in women's issues, such as one who is board-certified in women's health and/or psychiatric medications.

WHAT TO EXPECT DURING THE DIAGNOSTIC PROCESS

It is important to prepare for the diagnostic process. You may be asked many personal questions about childhood, relationships, and your current functioning. For some women, answering these questions can be difficult, but it can also be beneficial because it allows a psychiatrist to better assess the patient's overall functioning. Women with ADHD are encouraged to bring their partners, family members, or close friends with whom they feel comfortable discussing intimate details of their lives during the diagnostic process. By bringing supportive people to a psychiatric appointment, those with ADHD may feel more comfortable opening up and expressing what they are going through. However, it is important to remember that a psychiatrist doesn't need to meet all of a patient's loved ones. Instead, loved ones can help by reinforcing the best treatment strategies and strategies for coping with challenging symptoms.

Breathing Room

After receiving her initial diagnosis, women with ADHD should take advantage of "breathing room" where they can take some time to process what they have heard, go over any challenging symptoms and use the skills they have learned.

To get the best results, patients should get psychotherapy, including cognitive-behavioral therapy, interpersonal therapy, and psycho-education. Women with ADHD should also be involved in self-management programs and exercise, which effectively reduce symptoms. With treatment, symptoms of ADHD will likely decrease to the same level as a person without ADHD.

WHAT TO EXPECT AFTER THE DIAGNOSTIC PROCESS

When women receive their diagnosis, they should be prepared for changes in healthcare and medication options. The woman's insurance company may also require approval for necessary changes to treat ADHD, such as stimulant medications. With these changes in mind, women with ADHD should seek to manage their financial responsibilities by creating a budget and setting realistic expectations for themselves. Women with ADHD may have a hard time remembering these changes, which is why having a support system in place is critical. Having set expectations for yourself can also help you get a proper diagnosis, as you will be able to share more details about your life and name the symptoms you are experiencing. Once these symptoms are identified, it will make it easier to find a treatment that works best for you.

THE EFFECTS OF MISDIAGNOSIS

Getting a proper diagnosis is important, not only because it can lead to better treatment but also because it can help women understand themselves. Getting the right diagnosis can also benefit those who work with people with ADHD, such as family members, teachers, coaches, and employers. When women receive the right diagnosis, they can better support themselves and their loved ones.

Women with ADHD should not feel ashamed that they didn't already know they had the disorder. People with ADHD may not necessarily show the most obvious symptoms at a young age, thus making it harder to consider getting a diagnosis.

Help in Making the Diagnosis of ADHD in Women More Accurate

When diagnosing ADHD, women should identify behaviors that are not typical for them when they feel calm and in control. Women should also describe any time in their lives when they felt productive and effective. Describing these situations will help women explain what is happening for them when they feel overwhelmed or distracted, even during mundane tasks like cooking or driving. Knowing what helps to calm the symptoms of ADHD and what makes the symptoms worse can be very helpful in finding the best treatment strategy.

This is why it is so important for women with ADHD to have a support system throughout their journey in getting an accurate diagnosis. Having a support system in place will help with the emotional challenges that often accompany ADHD. The support system should be made up of family members, friends, or professionals who can relate to what women with ADHD are going through. This can help the woman advocate for herself while staying true to her needs and goals in life.

FINDING A SPECIALIST TO TREAT ADHD IN WOMEN

Once the diagnosis has been made, women with ADHD should promptly start getting treatment, which can be hard to do when these changes are so recent and challenging. Finding the right type of treatment will often take a lot of research, and finding an appropriate provider is important.

Because ADHD is a neurological condition, it's critical to find a provider who specializes in treating these conditions. By choosing an experienced provider, women with ADHD can ensure that their treatment will be effective.

Women with ADHD can also ask friends and family members to recommend someone they may have had a good experience with.

When looking for a provider, women with ADHD should ask several questions. Questions such as, 'Do you have experience treating adults or children?', and 'How long you have been treating adults with ADHD?' are important. It is also important to ask how frequently the provider will meet with you since treatment can include daily visits and regular telephone calls.

For women who don't have the time or resources to meet with their provider on a regular basis, choosing a provider who is willing to meet with them via phone or video is a great option.

Women with ADHD should expect that finding the right treatment will take time. There are no magic pills or overnight cures, but with time and dedication, they will reach their goals in life and improve their quality of life.

There are various different types of treatments available, and it is important to choose carefully to find one that can provide the best results for you. Knowing what each type of treatment entails will help you make a well-informed choice on which type would be best for your needs and lifestyle.

Suppose you are unsure of what type of treatment might work best in your life. An appointment with a psychiatrist who has experience in treating ADHD can help show you which treatment style and combination of medications will most likely work well for you.

It can also be helpful to ask your psychiatrist about treatment options for other mental health issues, such as anxiety and depression. Remember, however, that in order to feel more at ease in your surroundings and have fewer problems with your ADHD symptoms, you may require a different combination of medications or specific therapy.

If you find that the treatment plan and medications are not working at all, then it is possible that you do not have ADHD in the first place. If you suspect this is the case, seeing another psychiatrist is recommended so you can get the right relief for your symptoms.

The best way to take care of your mental health is to always talk with your healthcare provider. This will make it easier to find out what is wrong and what steps need to be taken next in order to feel better on a daily basis.

It's also worth noting that finding the right therapist can take some time. In general, people are not inclined to seek therapy or treatment on their own. However, if you take the time and do your homework, it will be easier for you to find a therapist who can give you the best treatment options possible.

In addition, it is critical that you communicate with your loved ones and let them know what's going on in your life and why it's so difficult to live with ADHD every day. They will likely be supportive and be more willing to work with you during this stressful period in your life if they understand what you are going through.

CHAPTER 10: NAVIGATING THROUGH A NEW DIAGNOSIS

When getting a diagnosis of ADHD, a woman may have mixed feelings about it. She may feel worried about her future since she has recently graduated and made a lot of progress in school, or she may also feel worried that others will judge her.

What is important for her to know is that her brain operates differently to most other people. It is not the result of mistakes or personal weaknesses, but rather it is due to having ADHD. While many women also experience personality disorders and mood disorders, it is estimated that over two-thirds of all women with ADHD are also considered to be neurotic (in other words, having a neurotic personality and mood).

Don't let this statistic deter you from seeking treatment. Falling into the stereotype of being a neurotic female is not helpful for you or anyone else. It's plausible that you need to reevaluate how much of your personality and behavior is influenced by your diagnosis. This diagnosis has shaped who you are today in a variety of ways, and it will also help shape the person you can become.

A NEW DIAGNOSIS

You may have been told that you are hyperactive, inattentive, or impulsive before, or maybe you have been told that your personality is different than most other people. When you get a diagnosis of ADHD, it means that this personality trait is now being considered a disorder. It may be hard to understand why ADHD is seen a problem instead of simply being a difference.

It's important to remember that no "norm" exists in every aspect of society. For example, many adults can sleep through the night without medication, while others cannot. Many adults don't have mood problems, and others have ongoing problems with depression and anxiety.

Even if you do feel different from others, it may be due to ADHD rather than a personality or mood disorder.

You may be feeling that you used to be fine, but now that you have been diagnosed with ADHD, your life is no longer fine. In most cases, this is just a result of early conditioning and learning. The events we experience growing up, and the reactions of others to these events offer us feedback about our behavior. In other words, we learn what we need to do to please others and how to react when confronted with new situations or difficult experiences.

If you think back on your childhood, you may remember that you had quite a lot of energy and were always eager to learn. In fact, you may have been considered hyperactive or impulsive at an early age, or maybe your parents or grandparents said that the most important thing they could give their child was a sense of responsibility. This can refer to a number of things, but it usually refers to the belief that children are born selfish and lazy and must be taught how to be good citizens.

Today, it is quite common for young adults to grow up in homes filled with rules, values, and expectations. If a child does not act appropriately toward her parents or others, she may come to believe that she no longer deserves love and support. In other words, she may feel like she is a bad person. This can cause her self-esteem to plummet and can result in depression and other problems.

However, the situation is not all bad. Since you have ADHD, you also have a different personality and temperament to most other people. In fact, when you have ADHD and are diagnosed properly, it can mean that you are more open to new experiences. As a result, you may be more forgiving and tolerant toward yourself as well as others when you receive the proper treatment and support.

In addition, having ADHD can mean that you are able to get along with a wide variety of people because of your ability to think about how others might feel. This is referred to as being empathic or intuitive. These traits may help build better relationships with your family members, friends, teachers, and employers.

You might also develop a more positive personality due to having ADHD. Instead of being directed by the expectations of others, you are more self-determined and have a more creative outlook on life. This may also make you more resilient and less likely to experience depression or anxiety.

MAKING THE DIAGNOSIS STICK

In some cases, you may need more information about ADHD before you feel comfortable enough to accept a diagnosis.

Since it is possible to have ADHD and also have other mental health issues, it is essential to have a clear diagnosis and treatment plan for both conditions.

It is also important to remember that if you continue to experience symptoms of depression or anxiety after regular treatment, this can mean that something else needs your immediate attention.

In most cases, medication and an ongoing treatment plan can help with your overall well-being, so it is essential to find the best psychiatrist who has experience in helping people with both ADHD and other mental health disorders.

COPING WITH A NEW DIAGNOSIS

People can react to their new ADHD diagnosis in different ways. It can be confusing, exciting, and upsetting all at the same time. Learning to manage the symptoms of ADHD and regain control over your life is a process that shouldn't be rushed.

It's also worth remembering that you're not alone in dealing with this problem and that a variety of professionals can assist you in figuring out how to best manage your symptoms.

When you're first diagnosed with ADHD, one of the best things you can do is openly talk about it with your friends and family. This can be helpful because they will already know what types of challenges you might face regularly and what they can do to help you live a healthier life overall.

Certain activities may not be possible for you when you are first diagnosed with ADHD, so make sure your loved ones know about these beforehand. This will help them understand your condition and not take it personally when you need to cancel plans on short notice or can't join them during the activity.

It's critical to spend time researching ADHD treatment options so you can figure out how to best manage your symptoms. Some medications are more effective than others, and some take longer for your body and brain to adjust to.

Additionally, there are therapeutic options if medication is not currently the best option for your needs. Instead of rushing into a decision about what type of medication or therapy that will work best, it is better to explore all of your options, taking into consideration how they will impact you in the long run. In most cases, you can continue using ADHD medications even if you are also having therapy on a regular basis.

If you're on ADHD medication, it's critical that you stick to your treatment plan if you want to get the most out of it.

It is also important to find out as much as possible about your diagnosis, what your options are, and how best to find support if needed. To get the most out of your medications, ensure that they are being taken consistently and at the right time each day.

It may be helpful for you to speak with someone who has gone through a similar ordeal in order to gain insight into the process.

If all of this knowledge makes you feel overwhelmed, speak with an expert who specializes in ADHD treatment. They will be able to help you explore your options and figure out which treatment will work best for your needs.

Currently, many different treatment options can help people with ADHD, including medication and therapy. In the past, medication was the only option for those who struggled with ADHD symptoms on a regular basis. However, with all the different treatments available now, it is possible to get the guidance you need from a professional who is committed to helping you live an overall healthier life.

FINDING TREATMENT OPTIONS

If you are unsure how to find the right type of ADHD treatment that can make your life better, it is important to ask your psychiatrist or therapist what their experience has taught them so far.

For instance, you may need to find a more effective pill for your needs. Finding the right treatment for ADHD can be difficult, so make sure you have the right medication before expecting any miracles.

If you are on medication and do not feel like it is working, it may be helpful to try a newer medication or a new dosage level. In many cases, people need a higher dosage level of their current medicine before they start to experience relief, so don't give up too soon.

While the placebo effect is potent and can temporarily improve your mood, it's critical to remember that taking the wrong ADHD medication can actually exacerbate your symptoms. If this occurs, your physician may wish to consult with you in order to determine the most appropriate medication for your particular circumstances.

Don't assume that one type of medicine can treat all your problems, particularly if you have been having problems with symptoms of ADHD for a long time. For instance, one type of medicine might be effective at treating depression, while another might help with anxiety.

It is also possible to find treatment options that combine medication with therapy. This can be very useful if you believe you are at risk of developing depression or anxiety.

Your psychiatrist may suggest going through therapy to learn coping skills. Therapy can help you develop healthy social skills and improve your self-esteem and confidence.

Along with experimenting with a few different options that may or may not work for you, you should also monitor any side effects associated with the medications you are taking.

As stated earlier, it is important to continue seeing your psychiatrist regularly to see how well your medication is working and making changes as necessary. In order to determine whether or not your medication is working as intended, make a list of signs and symptoms that have changed since starting your ADHD medication. If you continue to see the same signs and symptoms, it can be a sign that your medication needs to be adjusted.

It is important to continue the treatment plan for ADHD in order to experience the maximum benefit of your medicine. It can take some time for your body and brain to adapt to new medication, so you must remain committed to staying on track with this treatment plan for many months or even years. The last thing you want is to stop taking a particular type of medicine that has been helping you only to have a relapse in your symptoms.

An ADHD specialist can provide additional guidance on how to find the most appropriate treatment options. A specialized ADHD doctor can not only help you treat your condition but also help you learn how to manage symptoms of depression or anxiety in a healthy and productive way.

An ADHD specialist may want to work with your psychiatrist in order to find the best treatment options for your specific needs.

It is important to remember that any type of psychiatric treatment can be costly and may require more time than the majority of people are willing to invest. When you are ready to move forward with finding the best treatment options possible, however, the wait and expense may be well worth it.

Do not hesitate to ask your psychiatrist if they have any suggestions or recommendations for you when it comes to a particular treatment approach. Your doctor can help you find an effective ADHD treatment option that will lead to long-term relief and improve your quality of life.

Making an appointment with an ADHD specialist doctor can provide you with the tools you need to feel better as soon as possible. Understanding what is available to help people with this condition and how these treatments work will help you better understand which one might be best for you.

CHAPTER 11: STARTING THE THERAPEUTIC PROCESS

A critical part of the ADHD treatment process is starting ADHD medication. That said, be mindful that women may experience side effects when they first start taking medications, particularly if they are taking hormonal birth control.

Dr. Ghodsian, who specializes in treating women with ADHD, says that her patients generally notice a significant improvement in their symptoms after taking medication for several months. She recommends that women continue to take their medications for at least three to six months before making any changes. "Once you've stabilized on a good dose of ADHD medication, you can explore things like lifestyle changes and concurrent problems to help optimize your functioning," she says.

GETTING STARTED ON THE RIGHT ROUTE

Initial treatment for ADHD starts with a neuropsychological evaluation designed to assess the type of ADHD you have and learn your best treatment options. This is done by a psychologist or psychiatrist who works with adults with ADHD.

The evaluation usually includes administering a variety of psychological tests, including:

WAIS-IV (Wechsler Adult Intelligence Scale)

This is meant to test your basic learning abilities in various areas, including verbal comprehension, visual comprehension, and perceptual organization. It also tests your working memory, processing speed, and executive function.

ASRS (Attention-Deficit/Hyperactivity Disorder Rating Scale)

This test is used to determine the severity of your ADHD. It measures the way you respond to daily situations and asks you to rate your symptoms on a scale from 0 to 3. The test results are then compared against others who have been diagnosed with ADHD.

DSM-5 (Diagnostic and Statistical Manual)

This test focuses on the presence and severity of mental disorders, such as depression, bipolar disorder, schizophrenia, and PTSD. It also looks at all aspects of your social functioning.

WPT (Wisconsin Card Sorting Test)

This test measures how fast your mind can find the right card when placing them in their respective piles sequentially. The aim is to sort cards of different colors in an orderly manner quickly.

These tests will help develop a treatment plan and determine if any medications are needed. Your doctor may recommend you to start with a low dose of medicine and gradually increase it until you achieve the desired effect. It's important to be patient and persevere during this process, which could take several weeks.

TREATMENT CONSIDERATIONS FOR WOMEN

If you're going to take medication to treat your ADHD symptoms, talk to your doctor about the possible side effects. For example, if you are using hormonal birth control, ADHD medicines may interact with the hormones in birth control and could cause side effects. Your provider will likely recommend that you stop using hormonal birth control while taking ADHD medications. If you decide that you do want to continue using hormonal birth control, talk with your provider about which form of birth control would be best for your symptoms.

Another important topic when discussing medication is determining the right dosage. Women may need a lower dose than men, so be sure to discuss that with your provider. It's also important to note that you will want to take your medicine at the same time every day because ADHD medications are best absorbed by your body when taken in a consistent fashion. Consistent and regular dosages of ADHD medications can help reduce side effects, such as nervousness, severe mood swings, and difficulty falling asleep at night.

OTHER TREATMENT METHODS

Once you have started taking your ADHD medicine, you may notice things getting better in your life, but not all of your symptoms may be addressed. If this is the case, there are other choices for treating ADHD symptoms. These include:

Fitness

Exercise improves cardiovascular health and has many positive effects on brain chemistry, which can help reduce ADHD symptoms.

Stress-Reduction Techniques

Stress reduction techniques can help reduce ADHD symptoms. These techniques include deep breathing exercises, meditation, yoga, exercise, and even spending time in nature. The aim is to relax the body, mind, and emotions through different activities, not to cause anxiety or stress. By decreasing stress levels and increasing your sense of well-being, you can improve your overall mental health. It's essential to mention, though, that many of these techniques are geared toward self-improvement rather than ADHD treatment.

Emotional Support

It can be difficult to balance having ADHD with establishing and maintaining a family, pursuing your career, and having a social life. You may need to seek emotional support from friends and family to help you manage your symptoms. Make sure they know what kind of assistance you require so they can help you when you need it. It's also important to find support from others who are in the same situation as you. Through social media or other avenues, you can find resources designed for adults living with ADHD. Many support groups meet in person, which can be a great way to meet people who understand what it's like to live with ADHD and make new friends.

Diet

A high-fiber, low-sugar, high-protein diet has been linked to a reduction in ADHD symptoms. Decreasing caffeine intake can also prove helpful.

Although ADHD is a condition that many women suffer from, it is often overlooked and not talked about. By talking with your doctor or other health care providers, you can get the help you need to reduce symptoms and live a happier and healthier life.

SUPPORTING YOUR RECOVERY

One of the most important ways to cope with ADHD is to be patient and stick to your treatment plan. It takes time and practice, but it's crucial not to give up before you've tried everything you can. You can improve your outlook on life by learning to accept that you have ADHD and accepting that it is not a disability.

When it comes to ADHD, the key point to remember is that you are not alone. Many adults are living with the disorder, and there are people out there who understand what it's like to live with ADHD every day. Reach out to family and friends, seek professional help if necessary, and be honest about your feelings. You may not have control over your condition, but that doesn't mean you can't do things to help yourself live as well as possible with it.

GENERAL ADVICE FOR PARENTS AND CAREGIVERS

ADHD is not a child's disease. There are many adults struggling with ADHD because they were never properly diagnosed and treated as children. Parents and caregivers should begin to recognize and accept the signs of ADHD, particularly when it is more severe. The more parents and caregivers of children with ADHD become familiar with these signs, the more likely they will be able to detect the disorder before it gets worse.

Early detection of ADHD can improve the lives of not only those people who suffer from it but also those around them. Many people have ADHD, and it is sometimes difficult for them to function in normal society. This can lead to a variety of issues, including depression and social isolation. Therefore, it is important that the condition is treated effectively so it doesn't limit children's academic success.

It's also essential for parents to know that ADHD isn't always a lifelong issue. There are times when people diagnosed with ADHD as children "grow out" of it when they reach adulthood and experience less stress. However, there are other times when the disorder is more severe or has gone untreated, which prevents people from coping with life successfully once they enter adulthood. If a person has ADHD, the disorder can be treated successfully with the right treatment plan.

SPECIFIC ADVICE FOR WOMEN

As we have learned, women with ADHD are frequently misdiagnosed as having anxiety or depression, and they are often unaware of their condition until they reach adulthood. Women need to be diagnosed correctly because many have symptoms of depression, anxiety, and fatigue.

With proper treatment, it is possible to live a normal life with ADHD. However, many people with the disorder are embarrassed to seek help because of the negative stigma associated with it. This can lead to serious problems for the women who live with it. Women with ADHD need to be properly diagnosed and treated because the condition can be successfully managed with just a little effort on the part of the individual.

USING MEDICATION AS A TREATMENT OPTION

All adults with ADHD should consider using medication to treat their symptoms. Ritalin is a medication that is frequently prescribed to adults with attention deficit hyperactivity disorder (ADHD). It is a stimulant that primarily affects the part of the brain that controls behavior. When used properly, it can assist people with ADHD in maintaining attention, staying focused, and controlling their ability to make decisions.

However, these medications are not completely safe and effective for everyone who takes them. First, you need to make sure that you work with a doctor who understands ADHD and its effects. Secondly, you cannot simply take a pill or two when you have ADHD. You must be patient and stick with the treatment plan that your doctor gives you. You may be tempted to rely on medication alone, but it is important to remember that there are other ways to treat ADHD as well.

ADHD is often treated using medication because it is a serious condition that affects many people's lives. While these medications are not completely safe and effective for everyone who takes them, individuals should exhaust all other possibilities before giving up and concluding that medication does not work for them.

Stimulants have been used effectively to treat ADHD symptoms in children since the 1960s. However, more recent research suggests that they are most effective when paired with psychological treatment. In general, psychostimulants reduce hyperactivity and impulsivity while improving attention span and reducing distractibility.

Other drugs that are used to treat ADHD include:

- Adderall is a long-acting form of amphetamine. It is used to treat ADHD in adults who have not responded well to other forms of medication such as Ritalin or methylphenidate.

- Concerta is a non-amphetamine stimulant designed for children and has been shown to improve concentration and attention in adults with ADHD.

- Dexedrine is a non-amphetamine stimulant that is considered to be relatively safe. It's particularly effective in treating adults who have a combination of ADHD and substance abuse issues.

MEDITATION

Meditation is particularly useful to individuals with ADHD. A number of studies have shown that meditation can significantly improve mindfulness, attention, and executive functions. The capacity to be aware of what is occurring in the present moment, including your bodily sensations and emotions, is referred to as mindfulness. It also involves being sensitive to the effects of your thoughts on matters that are not actually happening at the moment. Attention can refer to how well you concentrate when listening to others, as well as being able to focus on your surroundings Executive functions are concerned with thinking in general. They are responsible for turning thoughts into actions and turning actions into concepts. Improvement in these areas is what allows individuals to do things in an intentional and organized way.

The following is how you can meditate at home:

- Make sure that you have a quiet place to meditate where you will not be interrupted.

- Make sure you are comfortable. It is recommended that you sit cross-legged on the floor if possible, but a normal sitting or lying position is fine as well.

- Focus on your breathing by taking deep breaths from your nose and letting them out through your mouth slowly, in tune with your heartbeat if possible.

- Focus on an object for about thirty seconds before moving your attention to something else in the room, then return to focus on the object once again after another thirty seconds has passed. (Do this until you notice that at least ten minutes have passed.)

- After you have completed your meditation session, sit in silence for at least five minutes to allow the effects of the meditation to fully take effect. (You may continue with this for as long as you like.)

- You can repeat this practice anywhere from five to ten times a day.

BEHAVIORAL THERAPIES

Behavioral therapy can help women with ADHD improve their focus and reduce their hyperactivity. It aims to empower the patient to compensate for their symptoms. It also teaches them problem-solving skills and other skills that can help them function better in life. Many communities have started to offer behavioral treatments through their community centers, free of charge. If you'd like to learn further about behavioral therapy, contact your local community center or a local therapist immediately.

TYPES OF BEHAVIORAL THERAPIES FOR WOMEN WITH ADHD

The key to behavioral therapy for women with ADHD is to find a therapist that they feel comfortable with and who understands each individual's needs. Look for a therapist that has experience working with those who live with ADHD.

Cognitive Behavioral Therapy (CBT)

In this type of treatment, the psychologist will identify negative thoughts and change them into positive ones. This can be done in therapy sessions or through homework assignments. In therapy, you may say things like, "I feel upset when my husband criticizes me for seemingly no reason." The patient will be asked to identify other examples of times when she is upset about something and then use that example to replace the negative thoughts towards her husband.

Cognitive Processing Therapy (CPT)

This type of therapy seeks to help people discover new ways of dealing with their problems and learn how to overcome their daily struggles in life through a combination of problem-solving therapies and cognitive restructuring techniques. The patient will learn to identify and dispute the negative thoughts about themselves, others, and their situations. They use cognitive puzzles to help patients understand themselves better and change their outlook on life.

Behavioral Activation (BA)

This type of therapy motivates the patient to increase positive activities in daily life and decrease negative behaviors. Rewards should be given for progress made towards decreasing the negative behaviors and increasing positive ones. Sometimes, these rewards can take the form of something simple, such as allowing patients to spend an extra hour with their kids or finding a hobby that they love. Often, patients need to be coaxed with positive reinforcements before making positive changes.

Dialectical Behavioral Therapy (DBT)

This type of therapy was developed for those with borderline personality disorder. It teaches patients about the importance of creating a "life worth living" and the skills that will help them do so. These skills are often used in conjunction with other therapies and treatments for ADHD. The therapist will teach self-regulation, mindfulness, distress tolerance, and emotion regulation skills. These pieces of knowledge can help women deal with their hyperactivity symptoms and their impulsive behaviors.

In-home Behavior Management

For those suffering from ADHD, it is important to be able to help themselves at home in order to stop their impulsive behaviors. Instead of working on their problems in therapy, they will work on keeping themselves focused and making positive changes while still at home. When the impulsive behavior begins, patients will stop what they are doing, find something else to do that doesn't cause them to act impulsively, and find some way to occupy their time until the mood is gone and they can return to normal. This can be hard because it requires a great deal of self-control and planning ahead. One of the few ways for those with ADHD to learn these skills is for them and their caregivers to work together on this type of therapy at home.

Social Skills Training (SST)

This type of therapy is used for those who have a hard time communicating with others and understanding how to interact with other people. The therapist will identify areas in which the patient may need improvement and then work on these issues through a series of assignments and homework. This is an active type of therapy that requires the patient to do more than sit back and listen to what the therapist is saying. Instead, they need to actively participate in various exercises such as joining groups and playing games with other people. This type of treatment is commonly used in conjunction with other behavioral therapies to assist individuals with ADHD in managing their behaviors and social skills.

Group Therapy

This type of therapy involves learning more about and communicating more effectively with other people. The therapist will help patients understand that social skills are behaviors that can be learned, just like any other skills. Social skills are learned through practicing new behaviors, conversing with real people, and reflecting on what you did wrong in conversation. This can include role-playing, feedback from a therapist or significant other, listening, eye contact, and communication training exercises such as mirror exercises.

Therapy groups are held by a therapist or treatment team. The therapy group is composed of other individuals who have

ADHD. They will meet with each other to learn about the different types of behavioral therapies that can help them manage their symptoms. Additionally, participating in a therapy group provides an outlet for sharing feelings and experiences with others who are coping with similar issues, reinforces treatment progress, and strengthens relationships with family and friends.

Self-Management Training (SMT)

This form of therapy is used to assist individuals with ADHD in managing their time. The therapist will have the patient keep a time log for 1–2 weeks and then have them analyze and discuss their results. The purpose of this exercise is for the patient to make positive changes in order to improve, which will result in increased success throughout adulthood.

Patient-Managed Support Groups

Patient-managed support groups are designed to provide ongoing support and socialization for individuals with ADHD who are self-managing their symptoms without the assistance of a therapist. The patient can take a leadership role in the group by organizing meetings, assigning tasks, and answering questions posed by other members. Many patients find it helpful to work through their problems together in a supportive environment instead of going through it alone at home or at work.

Behavioral therapy is extensively used in treating symptoms related to ADHD. Research has shown the effectiveness of the therapies.

Behavioral therapy works best when combined with other treatments. This is often done as a part of multimodal treatment. Stimulants, for example, improve attention and hyperactivity symptoms but have no effect on impulsivity and poor social skills, which behavior modification aims to address through substitution training (e.g., teaching children to keep their hands to themselves) and behavior contracting (e.g., rewarding appropriate behavior with privilege).

Behavioral therapies are often used in conjunction with medication treatment for people with ADHD. They can be especially effective for patients resistant to taking or who do not respond well to stimulant medications.

Behavioral therapies are also widely used to prevent the development of ADHD in preschool children who are considered at risk of developing it.

CHAPTER 12: GETTING THE APPROPRIATE SUPPORT

Getting the right support can be a challenge. It might be a too far away, hard to find, or too expensive. You might not even know what kind of support you need.

The challenges in finding help for attention deficit disorder affect both those with the disorder and those who try to support them. But getting the right support will help you lead a richer life with less stress and frustration.

The first step is to understand what kind of support you need. Remember that women are complicated. The support you need might be different from the kind of support a man would need.

There are several methods for obtaining professional assistance with ADHD:

1) Talk to your doctor(s).

Not all doctors know how to treat girls and women with this disorder – learn to customize a treatment plan based on the symptoms and priorities of a woman with ADHD.

2) Talk to a women's health professional.

Your doctor may not be able to tailor a treatment plan for you specifically, but your gynecologist or therapist can look at the symptoms of ADHD and match them with those that specifically affect women.

3) Talk to a psychiatrist.

Psychiatrists are experts in the psychology of girls and women, and many of them have treated patients with ADHD.

4) Join an adult ADHD support group.

There are various programs and sources of support for you, but they may be difficult to obtain or may not fit your lifestyle. The support you get in a group can be invaluable.

OVERCOMING STIGMA

ADHD is still a widely misunderstood condition. Millions of adults are undiagnosed or misdiagnosed and suffer without knowing why.

Stereotypes about people with ADHD prevent them from getting the help they need and living fulfilling lives. Here are three common misunderstandings and the truths behind them:

1) "ADHD is just an excuse."

ADHD is not a figment of the imagination; it has a biological basis in the brain. And, while some children with ADHD do outgrow their symptoms as they mature, many women with ADHD continue to have symptoms well into adulthood. These adults deserve to get appropriate treatment and support.

2) "Women with ADHD aren't as good as men."

Yes, women with ADHD are as good as men – perhaps even better. Individuals with ADHD are just as capable as the average woman to earn a doctorate. They're also more often leaders in their field.

3) "ADHD effects your worth as a person."

The effects of ADHD don't make someone a good or bad woman. ADHD is no less a part of the female experience than what makes you who you are – your personality, mood, identity, and values.

You can overcome these common misconceptions about women with ADHD by speaking the truth instead of letting rumors and misconceptions stand in your way. This will make people aware of the facts and help create a more supportive environment for your fellow sufferers.

Here are some other misconceptions you may face:

1. When you have ADHD, people hear "lazy" or "crazy."

You're not necessarily lazy or insane if you have attention deficit disorder; it's just that your brain is wired differently than most people. That makes it difficult for you to focus and pay attention like most people can and to get motivated to do so, but it doesn't mean that you're any less bright or thoughtful than anyone else.

2. It's shameful to admit that you have ADHD.

Admitting that you have attention deficit disorder is not shameful, no matter how much stigma surrounds it. Many women are diagnosed as adults and feel more motivated to get treatment once their children are in school. They get a second chance at life and now feel confident enough to do what they want.

3. ADHD is a phase – you'll grow out of it.

While it's likely that you'll grow out of its symptoms as you mature, by adulthood, many women with adult attention deficit are still dealing with symptoms of the disorder and therefore have to take medication.

4. Women don't need to be treated for ADHD because they're more well-rounded and successful than their male counterparts.

Women with ADHD are in the same situation as men with ADHD – they deserve the same excellent treatment that can help them live a full, rich life. The truth is that attention deficit affects both women and men but to different degrees based on individual factors like biology or upbringing. Women with ADHD deserve treatment that helps them function on a higher level.

5. Someone with ADHD can't raise a child as well as someone without it.

It's harder to meet all the needs of your child when you have attention deficit disorder, but you're still just as able to give the love and support that your child needs to grow into a healthy and successful adolescent and adult.

6. People with ADHD fail to take care of themselves because they don't take their medications or go to their appointments on time.

People with ADHD may not always take their medications, but that doesn't mean they don't want to improve and feel better or are not trying to take care of themselves. The medication sometimes makes them feel worse, which can deter them from taking it and going to their doctor appointments. It can be hard for women with ADHD to ensure they stay on top of the right treatments, so finding the right doctor can help you avoid this problem.

7. People with ADHD are bad parents because their kids are constantly in trouble at school.

If their parents have ADHD, their children are more likely to get into trouble at school because it is more difficult to manage a household and set boundaries for their children. Still, these behaviors are not caused by ADHD – there are other factors at play. Women with ADHD deserve the chance to get treatment for their disorder to be the best parents they can be.

MYTHS ABOUT WOMEN WITH ADHD

Being a woman and having an attention deficit is arguably harder than being a man and having it, but this doesn't make you any less deserving of support. To overcome these common hurdles, you need to know what you're dealing with first, so here's are a few common myths about women with ADHD:

- Women with ADHD are more sensitive and moody than women without it.

- Women with ADHD lose interest in themselves as they grow older.

- If you're a woman, you're less likely to get diagnosed with ADHD.

- There's no need to treat women for ADHD because it's just a part of being a woman, and our hormones make us moody anyway.

- Women who have children are less likely to get treatment for their ADHD than men who do so because they don't want their kids to know that there's something "wrong" with them.

- Women can't succeed in life if they have ADHD because they are irresponsible and self-absorbed more often than other women.

- Women with ADHD don't get to have the same level of success as men because they're not as hardworking, selfless, and driven.

- If a woman has ADHD, she'll leave her family in the dust and never be there for anyone.

- Women with ADHD can't be happy because they don't have the "attention span" to deal with their work or be successful.

- Being a woman and having ADHD is just a phase.

- The only time women should worry about getting treatment for ADHD is when their kids are at school. Otherwise, they shouldn't psychologically spend the time dealing with their ADHD because it isn't worth it.

Living with ADHD can be frustrating, but it doesn't mean that you can't learn how to manage your time and organize your life. Don't give up on yourself – find the best doctors in your area and get started on finding the treatment that works for you. It may be hard in the beginning, but you'll feel like a new person soon enough.

Women with ADHD deserve to be well-informed about their disorder and how it can affect their lives – don't let the negative stigmas associated with women and ADHD get in your way. Women with ADHD are strong, courageous, and want to thrive despite their disorder – they just need the right treatment to help them do so. Don't let anyone make you feel bad about yourself – you didn't ask for this disorder, but that doesn't mean that you can't learn to live a happy, healthy life. Allow others to see you for who you truly are.

CHAPTER 13: EMBRACING LIFE WHILE MANAGING ADHD

Women with ADHD often struggle to find enjoyment in what most people take for granted, like eating their favorite foods, making plans, and enjoying leisure time.

The following section will address common concerns about planning, self-care, and leisure activities that often result from living with ADHD:

- People who are not familiar with ADHD often believe that women should "just quit trying so hard" to function at the same level as people without ADHD. People who do not understand ADHD may suggest that it would be better to stop trying so hard and cut yourself some slack. The truth is that even when people put forth the effort, they frequently experience unexpected setbacks, despite their best efforts to manage the disorder.

- It is important for people with ADHD to balance their strengths and weaknesses; this is an ongoing process.

- People with ADHD tend to live in the present, where they want to be engaged and involved in what they are participating in rather than ruminating on past things or worrying about the future.

- People with ADHD tend to want to explore different options.

- They need to learn how to say "no." It is not always easy for the woman with ADHD to say, "I don't want to go out today," even when she feels as though she needs to stay home.

- It is very common for women with ADHD to have difficulty sleeping in rooms they do not feel comfortable in. They may be quite content with their own bedroom and sleeping arrangements, and it is entirely natural for them to become irritated when the bedroom is altered. They need to learn how to adapt to different conditions and environments.

- Many women with ADHD have a hard time doing

new things; however, they may be very creative in their work and express positive feelings about doing the same old thing repeatedly. In fact, for people with ADHD, it is often more difficult to do something new than to do something familiar.

- People with ADHD may feel agitated when they have to wait in line or stand still at an event. They hate feeling trapped or captive, so more often than not, they will try escaping from where they are supposed to be because it is too boring or tiring for them.

- It is common for women with ADHD to have difficulty self-regulating, especially when they are bored. They may not always be able to predict how they will feel or behave in the future; however, that does not mean that they should give up trying to anticipate changes in their moods and behavior. They can try making lists of different things they can do when they feel bored or restless.

- Many women with ADHD learn tricks to make up for the fact that their executive functions are impaired. Instead of changing who they are, they need to learn how to manage their time and energy.

- It is not uncommon for people with ADHD to become anxious, which may cause them to be very sensitive about anything that feels unusual. They tend to worry too much about insignificant things and then become frustrated when they cannot turn off their worries.

- Women with ADHD may think they have more problems than other people. Sometimes this stems from a negative bias they feel toward themselves, while other times, it comes from actually having more problems due to their struggles with ADHD. However, they can gain confidence in what they have by recognizing that they often have unique gifts.

- It is common for women with ADHD to feel inferior to their peers. They may assume that others are more socially or academically successful than them, although this is not always the case. In general, people with ADHD want to live up to the expectations of others and want those around them to be proud of them; however, they need to remember that everyone has different struggles in life.

FINDING YOUR GIFTS AND TALENTS

For some women with ADHD, socializing is a great source of pleasure and pride. They often enjoy being the center of attention and love doing silly things with their friends.

Though it can be difficult for them to stick to a conversation, they need to share what interests them with others without feeling shy or intimidated. It's okay for them to be themselves, even if people around them do not understand why they are different from others. Being different does not necessarily mean that they are defective; instead, they are unique.

They also need to be careful not to let what they are doing become overwhelming. They can do various with their friends that are fun and that help them learn new things, but they must make sure not to let these activities get out of control. Sometimes it is necessary to take a break from the things they enjoy doing. They need to learn how to share and balance themselves.

Many women with ADHD find it difficult to join or attend organizations, but this does not mean that they should give up on this path in life. They just need to focus on one thing at a time, then they can explore the new opportunities that arise through these activities and learn to share their passions and interests with others.

For some women with ADHD, finishing tasks can be challenging, especially when it seems difficult or tedious. They might lack the persistence or enthusiasm to finish things, but don't give up on them! While it may sometimes feel like an impossible task that will never end, perseverance is important and can be achieved through determination and good habits.

Many women with ADHD have a hard time staying focused both at work and at home. They tend to daydream, forget things, and get distracted easily. They need to make an effort to understand their learning styles and choose activities that will help them stay on track and organized.

Women with ADHD can struggle with taking tests, especially when they procrastinate or get overwhelmed by the thought of studying for an exam. They may experience anxiety before taking tests or find that they simply are not prepared because they cannot finish a seemingly boring task like studying. This is partly because they have trouble focusing on routine tasks, which can feel overwhelming and stressful.

Women with ADHD tend to have a hard time doing things the same way as their peers, which means they may set themselves up for failure. They need to embrace their unique style and enjoy the way they express themselves in life.

For some women with ADHD, paying attention is difficult. They tend not to follow directions, or directions may confuse them. This can be especially challenging when in school or when some new task comes up at work. They must ensure that their focus is appropriate and that they are not paying attention in the wrong way.

Some women with ADHD struggle with recognizing their weaknesses and strengths. Since they can be daydreamers, it's common for their good qualities to go unrecognized, especially if their focus is off in another direction or on something pointless or unimportant. They can use small steps to begin recognizing their strengths and working toward exercising these talents more often in life.

In today's fast-paced world, it can be hard for women with ADHD to find time to pursue hobbies they enjoy because they feel overwhelmed by the difficulty of getting things done. However, they must take time to do things that they enjoy. They can sit and relax more often or sneak in a little time for themselves here and there. It's okay to play around a little each day.

TOOLS TO HELP YOU SUCCEED AT WORK, SCHOOL, AND IN RELATIONSHIPS

While living with ADHD can be difficult, it does not have to be the end. With the right strategies, you and your loved ones can take your life back and live a more comfortable, productive life.

Women that suffer from ADHD are more likely to change employers frequently. ADHD sufferers frequently express a desire for variety and an eagerness to try new things. They may focus on a less competitive field such as freelance writing or self-employment to accommodate their various needs. They may also be more comfortable in short-term jobs or ones that don't require advanced degrees. Furthermore, ADHD adults may find that they are better suited to working at different times of the day. For example, they may do better working at night or on the weekend to avoid distractions and interruptions.

Finding an environment that fits your specific needs can be challenging but can result in greater productivity in the long run. It may require experimenting with different employment opportunities, but finding the right fit can help make a difficult situation more manageable.

IMPROVING YOUR ABILITY TO WORK WITH ADHD

Determine your personal strengths and weaknesses. There's no point in knowing what your ADHD symptoms are if you don't know what they mean to you! Take the time to list your strengths and weaknesses, both personally and professionally, so that you can start to leverage your strengths while working on ways to improve your weaknesses.

Establish support: Ask trusted family members or friends if they would be willing to help provide you with the support you need. Tell them how they can best help you in specific areas such as when being hyper-focused or overly distracted causes a problem for you.

Provide yourself with a structured environment: ADHD has been noted to cause difficulty in organizing, remembering, and being in control of one's thoughts. If you're often distracted, you may need to establish several areas for working. You may find that a desk at the front of your workspace is best to avoid distractions, such as people or even pets near your workspace.

Relaxation techniques: Relaxation techniques, such as guided imagery, can help you channel your attention, calm your mind, and quiet your hyperactive nervous system.

Take breaks: If it is difficult to focus and think clearly due to stress or anxiety, take a break where you can clear your head and unwind. Editing your work or doing other tasks during a break can also help to refocus attention on the task at hand.

Keep a record of your activities: A journal or planner can help you keep track of daily events, activities, and/or appointments. Writing things down can increase your memory and decrease stress by keeping you organized. It also assists you in being consistently productive.

Do regular exercise: Some people with ADHD find that exercise has a calming effect. Exercising regularly may also improve your ability to focus. Exercise also releases endorphins, which can help elevate your moods and reduce anxiety.

MAKE A PLAN TO STAY FOCUSED

Step 1. Write down all the tasks that you will need to complete to meet your goal for the day

1

____

2

____

3

____

4

____

5

____

6

____

Step 2. List these tasks in order of importance

1

____

2

____

3

____

4

____

5

____

6

____

Step 3. Identify the order in which you plan to complete your tasks and create a timeline with specific time frames for when each task should be completed.

12:00 pm-1:00 am _______________________________

1:00 am-2:00 am _______________________________

2:00 am-3:00 am _______________________________

3:00 am-4:00 am _______________________________

4:00 am-5:00 am _______________________________

5:00 am-6:00 am ____

6:00 am-7:00 am ____

7:00 am-8:00 am ____

8:00 am-9:00 am ____

9:00 am-10:00 am ____

10:00 am-11:00 am____

11:00 am-12:00 pm____

12:00 am-1:00 pm ____

1:00 pm-2:00 pm ____

2:00 pm-3:00 pm ____

3:00 pm-4:00 pm ____

4:00 pm-5:00 pm ____

5:00 pm-6:00 pm ____

6:00 pm-7:00 pm ____

7:00 pm-8:00 pm ____

8:00 pm-9:00 pm ____

9:00 pm-10:00 pm ____

10:00 pm-11:00 pm________________________________

11:00 pm-12:00 pm________________________________

Step 4. Complete the task within the time frame designated by your timeline.

Step 5. Evaluate: Was each task completed with ease or difficulty? How can you adjust your timeline accordingly for future tasks?

1

____

2

____

3

____

4

____

5

____

6

____

WAYS TO MANAGE ATTENTION DEFICIT

Women with ADHD often have a hard time staying focused, especially when they are dealing with certain issues that could cause stress or anxiety. Although the symptoms of ADHD can be experienced in other areas of one's life, such as schoolwork, friendships, and romantic relationships, there tends to be a particular manifestation in challenging situations.

The following are some suggestions to assist you in maintaining your focus on the task at hand. Consider the following suggestions for coping with ADHD:

If you're dealing with an overwhelming situation, such as ongoing frustration or a continual irritant, then it may be necessary to deal with it later, once you've had a chance to sort through your thoughts and calm yourself down.

Maintain a steady supply of "on task" thoughts. If you are constantly switching from one thought to another, it is almost impossible for you to focus on the task at hand. Maintain focus on a single task until it is completed.

When you're thinking of something to do, don't get sidetracked. Don't say to yourself, "I'll think about that later." If there's a thought that pops into your head and you start thinking about it instead of completing the task at hand, then it is much more difficult to stay focused.

Try not to procrastinate. Make sure you get started on your work right away instead of putting it off and doing it later.

PLAN TO MANAGE ATTENTION DEFICIT

Step 1. Identify the tasks that you are having difficulty completing.

1

____

2

____

3

____

4

____

5

____

6

____

Step 2. Write down the steps involved in completing each task:

1

____

2

____

3

____

4

____

5

____

6

____

Step 3. Record the time spent on each task:

1

____

2

____

3

____

4

____

5

____

6

____

Step 4. Write your timeline and note how often you procrastinate on tasks.

1

____

2

____

3

____

4

____

5

____

6

____

Step 5. Evaluate: Was each task completed easily or were they difficult? How can you adjust your timeline accordingly for future tasks?

1

____

2

____

3

____

4

____

5

____

6

____

If you find that you are always procrastinating, consult your doctor. They may have recommendations for how to make sure that you are on task and stay that way throughout the day. If your ADHD symptoms are severe, they may have you start using a stimulant such as Ritalin or Adderall to help manage your attention.

PART 4 - THE CHALLENGES OF ADHD

CHAPTER 14: THE DIFFICULTIES OF ADHD THAT GOES UNDIAGNOSED

I t can be difficult to understand what it's like to have ADHD if you've never been diagnosed with the condition. This is especially critical for women who are frequently misdiagnosed with depression or anxiety. Because of this ignorance, many family members and coworkers may feel compelled to comment on your performance and pass personal judgments on your competence based on their limited understanding of the disorder. Unsurprisingly, these interactions can lead to feelings of shame and isolation.

However, once a woman has received an ADHD diagnosis, she and her loved ones can work together to find ways of coping. Encouraging the person with ADHD to seek treatment is often a good place to start. Moreover, it can be helpful to let the woman with ADHD know that her performance isn't her fault.

For instance, once a woman was reprimanded by her boss for going too slow on a project. Rather than allowing the incident to affect her, she reminded him that if he wanted her to work faster, he should give clearer instructions and avoid standing over her shoulder.

When she did this, he immediately backtracked on his criticism, apologized for his behavior, and genuinely thanked her for explaining the process to him. She had been correct that he was looking at everything from his perspective and not considering hers. This is often a common pattern for men whose wives or partners are diagnosed with ADHD. Once they learn more about the disorder and its symptoms, they're able to see their loved ones' performance through new eyes — eyes that don't characterize ADHD symptoms as personal flaws instead of as brain differences.

Some women with ADHD may feel that their loved ones and co-workers are being too hard on them or being too critical. If a woman makes a mistake, it can be easy for her to go down the rabbit hole of negative self-talk, leading to the feeling that she's not good at anything. She may feel as if she has been unfairly singled out to take responsibility for everything that goes wrong in her life. Rather than stand up for herself when faced with unjust criticism, she might bend over backward to try to please everyone else so that they'll stop criticizing her work ethic or belittling her abilities.

But by learning how to compensate when she feels overwhelmed, women with ADHD may find that they can perform at a higher level. For example, once a woman was told by her boss that she was on track for having the worst performance review of anyone in their department for several years straight. She was given feedback from the director and the human resources manager that no precedent existed for such a review in their company, which meant that she would be fired if she didn't get her act together fast.

However, the woman had just been diagnosed with ADHD and was taking medication for it. Once she started treatment, her focus improved, her energy level increased, and her ability to connect the dots increased. In short, she managed the symptoms of ADHD by using what she had learned from her therapist and psychiatrist. As a result of those improvements in her symptoms, the woman's performance lived up to the expectations of both HR and management. Her raised spirits contributed to this success as much as any other factor.

If you have ADHD and know that it's affecting your ability to perform, try to shift your perspective on what's been happening in the workplace. A woman with the disorder can often find ways of compensating for her symptoms. This can be done by learning strategies that help you focus and manage the fatigue that many women with ADHD experience during the day or by setting aside some time each week to practice relaxing. Knowing what you need to do to compensate for your symptoms, or at least take better care of yourself while they're still present, you'll find it easier to focus when you're at work — which is a requirement if you want to get ahead professionally.

In addition, it may be beneficial to set aside some time each day to reflect on how you got to where you are in your career and what the most difficult aspects of working for your employer have been. Once a woman understands the challenges she faces at work, she will know what she needs to do to beat them and get ahead. This can help her avoid feeling hopeless or like a failure when things don't go as planned.

Women with undiagnosed ADHD may struggle with their interpersonal relationships without knowing that they're struggling. They may believe they are constantly falling short of their loved ones' expectations or that they are unable to match the pace of those around them. Before the woman is diagnosed and takes medication to control her symptoms, this feeling can become even more overwhelming. Even after diagnosis, some women may go through stages of denial as they work to validate their condition. Yet having ADHD doesn't mean that a woman can't have loving relationships or keep up with the pace of life around her.

THE IMPACT OF ADHD ON THE FAMILY

Many women with undiagnosed ADHD may find that their symptoms negatively impact their relationships with family members. Because women with ADHD often have difficulty managing their emotions, they can become impatient and angry when a situation doesn't go as planned. If a woman responds to her family members' comments and offers while processing her thoughts, she might make a wrong assumption about what they're trying to say. For example, she might assume that her sister is asking for help with her housework when she wants to talk about something else entirely.

If a woman goes into these situations in an agitated state of mind, this may cause problems. Instead of interacting with them like an adult, the woman might become short-tempered and lash out at them in response to their comments or questions. She might even perceive her loved ones' comments as attacks meant to belittle her.

The woman may have trouble recognizing these and other signs that her family members are angry, and may feel that she's being blamed for something that isn't real. She might feel compelled to defend herself, which only makes matters worse. When this happens in a mixed company, it can cause a lot of damage to a woman's career if those with whom she works know how poorly she deals with conflict.

A woman with ADHD might also find that she has trouble giving her loved ones the attention they need or deserve. Although she might mean well, the woman can neglect her family's needs due to her ADHD symptoms. She may not have time to take care of them when they're sick or make time for them in her busy schedule. A woman with ADHD who has children, for example, may choose to take on too many tasks around the house rather than spend time with her children. She might also be so preoccupied with work and other responsibilities that she forgets about their extracurricular activities, or doesn't see how important it is for their health and growth to participate in them.

To avoid a scene or falling short of her family's expectations, she might be tempted to give her loved ones the cold shoulder. In doing so, she might affect the development of her children by depriving them of the attention they need to feel connected and secure. She may also overestimate the benefits of spending time with them and become frustrated when they don't show her how much they love spending time with her.

Sometimes this behavior is linked to social anxiety, which arises from a belief that someone will find out about a particular secret or embarrassment and take revenge against one's family due to that knowledge.

Because family life can be stressful for a woman with undiagnosed ADHD, she may become resentful towards others without realizing this resentment exists. The woman might then miss important life events or make comments that hurt others' feelings without realizing it. Although she may feel justified in judging the actions of others based on the way she feels, she can't know what's going on inside their minds and bodies.

For example, a woman with ADHD might believe her husband is having an affair when he spends more time at work than usual. To avoid being hurt, she might become vindictive towards him by finding ways to make his life uncomfortable. She may do this without realizing that she's doing it and without understanding why she's doing it. The woman might end up badgering her husband about his whereabouts or bringing up the subject during arguments.

Like many women with undiagnosed ADHD, this woman might assume that others are plotting to get back at her for something she did. Yet when she doesn't take notice of the clues her husband sends her, she doesn't realize how cruel she's being and how hurtful her behavior is to him. This can make it difficult for the woman to let go of the anger in order to work through any problems in the relationship. If her actions continue, they might end up separating or having affairs.

THE ADHD WOMAN AND HER LOVED ONES

As mentioned previously, symptoms of undiagnosed ADHD can impact nearly every aspect of life for a woman with ADHD. Her impact on her family members is often as severe as her symptoms and can be just as difficult for them to deal with.

The woman with ADHD may be the one who brings up issues when it's best for everyone else in the relationship to let them go. This can make the best of relationships seem excruciating, but this situation isn't unique to women with ADHD. It happens in every relationship, even though women are more likely than men to have this problem.

The woman with ADHD might find that her loved ones begin to find her behavior irritating and even threatening. This can cause the woman a slew of problems because it makes it difficult for others to respond to her needs or get along with her. This can cause the woman's family members to become frustrated and angry at her, which is often a result of how she treats them. The woman may not realize how her behavior has affected those in her life.

Even if a woman with ADHD is aware of these symptoms, she may become resistant to getting help for them because she believes that doing so will destroy her previously good reputation in the eyes of others. Psychologists can help with this by helping women with ADHD understand how common these symptoms are and how to minimize their impact on others. When people with ADHD understand how others feel about them, they're more likely to get the help they need from therapists and counselors.

Many women with undiagnosed ADHD are not consciously aware of the challenges they face in getting along with others. If those around them blame each other for their problems or can't communicate their needs, it can be easy for them to decide that their relationship is doomed from the start – and that it's probably not their fault. Yet this conclusion is based on individual circumstances that aren't exclusive to women with ADHD. It can happen in any relationship, yet women are more likely than men to blame themselves for past mistakes and take responsibility for making up for what happened in the present and future. This can make determining whether or not their relationship is progressing difficult.

A woman with ADHD might find that her loved ones begin to feel irritated or even threatened by her behavior. This can cause plenty of issues for the woman because it makes it difficult for others to respond to her needs or get along with her.

ATTENTION AND BEHAVIOR WHILE DRIVING

Some women with undiagnosed ADHD may find that they're most likely to take risks or do things that could lead to an accident when they're driving. This is just one example of how undiagnosed ADHD can impact a woman's choices and decisions during her life. The same risk taking can also apply to decision-making skills during other stages of life, including marriage, child-rearing, and choosing a career path. Although events may start turning for the better for a woman with undiagnosed ADHD when she reaches certain milestones, like having children or getting married, these moments may be overshadowed by issues that arise because she doesn't know how to manage her symptoms.

Many women with undiagnosed ADHD may think they're doing something good by trying to defeat distractions while they're driving. For example, a woman may believe she is doing the right thing by telling herself she won't listen to the radio or talk on the phone while driving because she is afraid she will be tempted to do one or both.

However, ignoring all the warning signals around her can make it harder for her to understand and manage those situations she should be aware of. This means that she could be driving under dangerous circumstances, which can affect her ability to stay in control of her car. All of this can put others at risk of being injured or killed.

CHAPTER 15: THE DIFFICULTIES OF UNTREATED ADHD

U ntreated ADHD presents unique challenges for those living with the disorder, and their loved ones.

Untreated ADHD sufferers are often extremely hard on themselves. They may feel angry or anxious, or frustrated that they can't seem to accomplish what other people find simple. They might spend hours organizing their workspace only to have it undone in minutes due to lack of focus. This same lack of focus can have major consequences for time management and relationships.

ADHD sufferers who don't get treatment tend to isolate themselves because they are often so wrapped up in self-blame, anger, and frustration that they are unable to interact with others in healthy ways. Their relationships with their children, friends, and significant others can suffer greatly as a result.

Although we all experience stress or unhappiness, untreated ADHD is one of the more challenging mental health problems to overcome because it is lifelong and requires ongoing attention. Treating ADHD requires having an open mind about which factors contribute to the development of the disorder and how you can manage them or help your family members manage them. It requires a firm understanding of ADHD itself.

ADHD sufferers who don't get treatment will often have difficulty in the following areas:

1. Physical Health

This can include many health issues, including obesity, high blood pressure, lack of sleep, tobacco use, and so on. Treatment centers around getting the patient to a healthy weight and living in a healthy environment. Most people with untreated ADHD have difficulty making healthy and sustainable lifestyle choices.

2. Education

Most people with untreated ADHD had problems in school during their childhood. These problems cause frustration that often leads to quitting or dropping out. Some will also have problems with learning as adults. Note that this is not true of all people with ADHD, but it is true for many.

3. Employment

Most people with untreated ADHD have problems in the workplace, often quitting or being fired. Untreated ADHD can also lead to problems with supervisors, as people with ADHD tend not to have the tolerance level needed for working under someone else.

4. Marriage/relationships

Most people with untreated ADHD have marital problems and difficulties in their relationships with others. This area is often fraught with resentment, lack of communication, and an inability to experience intimate relationships.

5. Finances

People who do not treat their ADHD often have difficulty managing their finances; they are likely to charge everything on credit cards without any self-control and will then have difficulty paying them off. They may even steal or get into legal trouble.

6. Risk-taking

Untreated ADHD patients are more likely to take unnecessary risks, such as driving too fast out of boredom. They also have a higher rate of accidents, injuries, and death than the general population.

7. Mood Disorders

These can include depression or anxiety and are often related to stress or family problems at home. Untreated ADHD can cause mood disorders even if they previously did not exist.

8. Social problems

Most people with untreated ADHD have problems interacting with others and difficulty following rules that other people follow without thinking about it (i.e. being on time, appropriate social behavior, etc.)

9. Self-esteem

Untreated ADHD can cause low self-esteem and feelings of inadequacy.

10. Legal problems

People with untreated ADHD may find it difficult to follow the law, often being arrested and/or pleading guilty to crimes they did not commit.

11. Eating disorders

Untreated ADHD can lead to eating disorders like anorexia or bulimia, which contribute to major health problems.

12. Disease susceptibility

Because of their inability to focus on what is going on around them or the consequences of their actions, people with untreated ADHD are more likely to contract a variety of diseases. They also have a hard time following through on treatment due to their distractibility.

13. Dependent personalities

People with untreated ADHD tend to develop dependent personalities as they get older. They tend to be less responsible than the general population, often letting others take care of them even when they can take care of themselves.

14. Use of drugs and alcohol

Untreated ADHD often leads to alcohol and drug use problems. Many people who do not treat their ADHD will begin abusing alcohol and drugs in a desperate attempt to manage their thoughts, or will use them because they have no other coping mechanism.

15. Suicidal tendencies

Untreated ADHD can contribute to an increased likelihood of suicide attempts.

16. Violence

People with untreated ADHD often have little impulse control and are more likely to commit major acts of violence, such as mass shootings. They're also more likely to be apprehended or killed in a shooting spree.

THE IMPACT OF ADHD ON RELATIONSHIPS

Women with ADHD often have a hard time in relationships due to their ADHD.

Some women with untreated ADHD have sexual compulsions, promiscuity, or an inability to control their sexual urges and desires. They may also have problems with pornography addiction or use it to relieve their boredom.

Lack of impulse control often leads them into dangerous sexual situations or one-night stands that lead to long-term problems in their relationships.

Some women with untreated ADHD who are married or in long-term relationships will cheat on their partners; this can lead to the end of a relationship and sadness for all involved.

They may also suffer physical abuse and violence, leading to personal injury, hospitalization, and even death.

People with untreated ADHD tend not to understand that their behavior is destructive and upsetting to others in their lives. This can lead to estrangement from family members, divorce and chronic loneliness.

Women with untreated ADHD often have a harder time relating to other women due to their problems communicating, controlling themselves, and understanding other people's needs.

Similarly, many women will experience relationship difficulties if they are married to or living with someone who has untreated ADHD and cannot have a healthy relationship.

Parents with untreated ADHD often have poor relationships with their children, leading to unruly youngsters who are difficult to control, exhibit inattention and a lack of concentration at school, and are frequently in trouble with teachers.

People with untreated ADHD can also have trouble relating to animals, sometimes leading them to abuse animals or ignore pets' needs altogether.

They will also often have relationship difficulties at work, leading to lower performance and job dissatisfaction.

Women with untreated ADHD can have trouble relating to their mothers, sisters, or other female relatives since they seem unable to relate to others. They are often rejected by their female relatives and may also have trouble relating to female teachers or bosses due to their inability to control themselves in certain situations. This can lead to difficulties as they seek work or try out for teams.

THE CHALLENGES OF UNTREATED ADHD

Life is a series of challenges, and women with ADHD may have more difficulty overcoming those challenges. Untreated ADHD can lead to the following:

1. Memory problems

Women with untreated ADHD often have issues with memory problems, usually in short-term memory.

2. Distractibility

Women with untreated ADHD also have trouble concentrating. They often have difficulty at school, work, in family life, and in other social situations.

3. Impulsive behavior

Women with untreated ADHD often behave impulsively because they are unable to think ahead before acting or second-guessing their current thoughts or feelings. This can result in risk-taking behavior that is dangerous for themselves and others. They may also engage in risky sexual behavior and substance abuse due to the need to cope with their rapid emotional changes.

4. Poor self-esteem

There are many reasons for women with untreated ADHD to have low self-esteem. Many feel that they are not as smart as their peers and may have trouble relating to other people. Many of them fail in school, work, or relationships due to their inability to control themselves, follow through on plans, and concentrate on the task at hand. Low self-esteem is a common problem among untreated ADHD sufferers since they have so much difficulty with everyday life.

5. Poor social skills

Women with untreated ADHD often have little to no social skills due to their being unable to read social cues. This can lead them into many dangerous situations that could have been avoided. This is especially true for women who feel as though they are less attractive than other girls or women, have trouble relating to their female relatives, or are married to someone who doesn't understand them.

6. Impulsivity

Women with untreated ADHD can also be impulsive may and make decisions based on the moment rather than thinking long-term about the consequences of their actions. For example, they may decide to start smoking or stop taking medications because they think it will be better for them.

7. Lack of concentration

Women with untreated ADHD often have trouble concentrating on the task at hand, whether it is taking a test, reading a book, listening to a teacher speak in class, concentrating on an important conversation, or solving relationship problems with family and friends.

8. The need for immediate gratification

Women with untreated ADHD also have trouble delaying their gratification; they usually don't deal well with lessons that involve procrastination or delayed rewards. They are also likely to have trouble waiting for their turn in conversation or situations and will have poor patience.

9. Difficulty with time management

There is a clear link between being able to manage your time effectively and performing well on timed exams, projects, or presentations. Women with untreated ADHD often struggle with time management due to the fact that they cannot be patient while waiting for things. It can take them longer than normal to complete tasks because they tend not to know how long things will take.

10. Difficulty with self-control

Women with untreated ADHD often have trouble resisting their impulses. They often have a sense of moral failure and guilt if they do something that they know is not in their best interests or the best interests of others but cannot control themselves, and do it anyway.

11. Difficulties in marriage

Many women with untreated ADHD also report difficulties within their marriage due to their behavior and personality. This could be due to a lack of trust in their spouse, or a husband who does not understand ADHD, among other factors. They also may feel as though they do not deserve a good relationship or that they are not good enough for their partner.

12. Difficulty with motherhood

Untreated ADHD can also lead to difficulties with motherhood. A woman with ADHD may have trouble relating to her child, being present, and being able to get them to school or activities on time. She will have trouble getting work done and doing things at home while she is taking care of a baby.

13. Ulcers

Many women with untreated ADHD have ulcers that cause stomach problems, especially during stressful situations such as school tests, work, or driving.

14. Difficulty sleeping

Accidents, injury to themselves and others, job loss, and other consequences can result from a failure to think things through before acting. These can be very stressful situations for women with ADHD. It can lead to insomnia and difficulty concentrating on other tasks or even reading a book at night due to being overstimulated from the day's events.

15. Learning problems

When women with untreated ADHD have trouble concentrating in class, they struggle to retain what their teachers say; therefore, they take longer than most students to study for tests. Women with untreated ADHD also have a hard time organizing their notes due to the fact that they cannot stay on task during class discussions or lectures.

16. Frequent headaches/stomach aches

Many women with untreated ADHD say they get frequent headaches as well as stomach aches. This may be due to the amount of stress they are under and the fact that their body is not coping with it.

17. Feelings of loneliness/being misunderstood

Many women feel alone and misunderstood by others who do not have ADHD. Others may not understand why they act the way they do, making them feel as if they don't deserve friends or love.

18. Poor decision making

For many women with untreated ADHD, poor decision-making is simply a part of everyday life. This makes them feel as though they don't have the same control over their lives as those who do not have ADHD.

19. Procrastination

Many women with untreated ADHD also suffer from procrastination and setting limits on the number of things that are possible for them to accomplish in a day or week. They may feel as though they need to do more than is possible because they constantly feel as though they are falling behind.

20. Balancing their needs with those of others

Many women with untreated ADHD struggle with balancing their own needs with those of others. They often find it difficult to decide the best course of action at any given time.

21. Trouble keeping secrets

Women with untreated ADHD may have a hard time keeping secrets. This can make them very uncomfortable in social situations that involve dealing with others' secrets and can lead to them not being trusted by friends and family.

22. Intimacy problems

Women with untreated ADHD often have trouble with intimacy. They are likely to have trouble expressing themselves verbally and having serious discussions with partners, preferring small talk and joking around.

23. Trouble maintaining friendships

Women with untreated ADHD often have difficulty keeping friends because they have trouble making decisions and completing tasks. This is due to their inability to stay focused during conversations and other situations.

24. Being easily distracted

Many women with ADHD say that they love learning new things. However, many also say they are easily distracted by the world around them, making it hard to focus on the information they are trying to retain.

25. Problems with writing/reading comprehension

Because many women with untreated ADHD have difficulty focusing in class and studying, they also find it difficult to write or read comprehension questions and texts. They may also report having a hard time helping their children with their homework for this reason.

As you can see from the above list, there are many challenges faced by women who suffer from untreated ADHD. It is imperative that this disorder is recognized and treated as quickly and efficiently as possible so that the women who suffer from it can begin to lead healthier and happier lives.

CHAPTER 16: COPING WITH A WOMEN WHO HAS ADHD?

It can be hard to live with a woman with ADHD. "Who is this person?" you might wonder, as you try to figure out how to best support her. She transforms from one minute to the next, as if she were a chameleon changing colors in response to her surroundings. She may do things easily one day and have no idea how to do them the next. For example, if it's a smooth morning at home with her children and husband, everything might appear to be working perfectly. But then she arrives at work and feels completely out of sync with the rest of the world.

It can also be hard for her to live with someone else, as she struggles daily with self-determination and self-advocacy skills. She may feel that the two of you can't agree on anything, whether that be going to the store or cooking dinner. Breaking the pattern of arguing, frustration, and sadness is the first step in understanding who she is.

Every minute of every day, she may feel that she is an alien from another planet who doesn't belong. She may cry and ask herself why nothing seems to make sense. She may feel that no one has ever been or will ever be like her again.

Walking on Eggshells

ADHD can make your partner seem like a "Jekyll and Hyde" character, with her moods changing depending on her emotional state and what's happening in the family or at work. She may be your primary support system and the source of much pride, but in her state of hyperactivity and inattentiveness, she can be a stormy force.

It's important to remember that she usually feels very strongly about things. This might lead you to feel that she is aggressive or insensitive and that it's hard to talk to her.

ADHD causes particular problems during times of extreme stress. If you get into a fight with her and feel hurt or rejected, she may believe she is powerless to change. You may have to work on your relationship together.

Over time, you may find that your patience is wearing thin and that you're getting tired of her outbursts and short-temper.

You might also start blaming yourself for any problems in the marriage. You may even believe that leaving her is the only way to improve your situation.

But you can't afford to give up on her because she needs you as much as you need her. You need to stay connected to each other and maintain a sense of humor about the difficulties in your relationship. Otherwise, you might both feel too overwhelmed and be tempted to ignore or avoid each other. That isn't going to help either of you.

What You Can Do

Learn to be more direct and honest about your feelings. It's hard for her to move from one mood to another, so you'll have to help her. For example, let's say you work together, and your boss asked you to work on a project together. She could be overwhelmed, which would explain why she hasn't finished the task at hand, or done well with her work.

In a situation like this, try not to get angry. Anger will only make her feel bad about herself, which will lead to more mistakes, anger, and frustration. You need to help her identify times when she doesn't feel good and try to help her find ways through it. Find ways to break the pattern. And remember not to take her outbursts personally. The fact that your partner has ADHD is not a reason for either of you to give up on each other.

ACCEPTING THE DIAGNOSIS

The diagnosis of ADHD can be a relief to many, as it brings a level of understanding. However, ADHD can be very debilitating, causing a high level of stress in people with and without the condition. You may have trouble understanding your partner's ADHD symptoms and how it affects her life. It can take some time for you both to fully heal after the initial shock of the diagnosis and to find out the best ways forward.

Often, sufferers might also need some time to recover from the strain of being diagnosed. It's important to support each other in learning how to manage the condition, so it doesn't become a source of stress for either of you. If you don't feel you can do this together, it may be a good idea to seek out someone who can help you communicate better.

If your partner is adamant about her viewpoints, it may be best to trust her and pay attention to what she has to say. But if she doesn't want to discuss what's on her mind, it can be helpful for you to propose your ideas or research something alone to understand the issue better. This will help you understand her better and find ways to sync up with her.

Support each other's efforts to accept the diagnosis and change your habits. For both of you, coming to terms with the diagnosis can be an emotional, frustrating, and exhausting experience. It is important to continue communicating as you work through your feelings. You can also learn to work together as a team and find a way to accomplish positive things together. Getting started may be difficult, but you'll feel much better once you do.

Getting Help

You can help each other by learning about ADHD and working on your relationship issues with a therapist. A therapist will help you identify ways to improve your relationship. They can also work with you individually to help you manage the stress of what's happening in your lives. This is important to do now before life becomes even more difficult for you both.

There are a number of therapists that specialize in treating re-lationships and ADHD. Search the Internet for one near you, or ask your doctor for a referral. Your doctor may also be able to point you in the direction of support groups that deal with relationships and ADHD. These days, there is so much in-formation available that no one should have to endure their struggles alone.

However, if you don't currently have a therapist for whatever reason, it doesn't mean you can't manage on your own. You can learn more about ADHD and its effect on relationships by studying research literature and talking to other people who have been through the same challenges. Learn from their mistakes, successes, and strategies. It's certainly a better start than suffering in ignorance for years.

DEALING WITH PRIDE AND SHAME

Your partner has ADHD, and you don't. You may think she is stubborn and difficult to deal with because she has this disorder. She may feel ashamed of her behavior and think she's hopeless, and that there's no point in even trying. She might even feel that she's a failure.

These kinds of problems can be hard to deal with, but you can help each other overcome them by taking small steps. You can share your feelings and how they affect you in a kind and compassionate way. Additionally, you can learn more about ADHD on the Internet or even talk to someone else who has ADHD. You and your partner will both feel more comfortable you better understand the condition.

You may need to work on overcoming your pride and shame to get the help you both need. Don't have to assume that your partner's ADHD is a result of her poor behavior or mistakes. Understanding the impact of ADHD on an individual's choices, rather than simply punishing them, will be more productive for both of you.

Accepting that she acts differently because of ADHD and not because she's lazy or lacks intelligence will free her from feeling guilty about her actions. Remember that it may take her extra effort to do things the way you or anyone else want or expect them to be done, so give her a break. Doing so doesn't mean that you're giving up on your standards, but it will help you understand how to work together without unnecessary stress.

CHAPTER 17: WORKING WITH WOMEN DIAGNOSED WITH ADHD

As we have mentioned previously, women with ADHD may face many challenges in life and at work. They often feel misunderstood and unsupported by others who believe they are not putting in the effort like everyone else.

A woman may have trouble focusing on one task, and her working memory is often poor, so forgetfulness can be a huge problem. She may have trouble transitioning from one task to another, resulting in incomplete tasks and frustration from colleagues and bosses. She may fail to recognize the impact of her work on others or have difficulty following through. She may be disorganized, which can lead people to believe that she is lazy and just making excuses.

A woman with ADHD may jump from one project to another. This makes it hard for her to complete tasks which causes frustration in both herself and others around her. She may need more time and help to complete tasks than her colleagues.

A woman with ADHD is often hyperactive, impulsive, and overly emotional. She may be described as defiant. She may be more likely to show anger, resist social rules, and seek thrills and stimulation. Her impulsivity can lead her to serious problems with the law or her personal life. A lack of empathy can make it difficult for her to understand the feelings of others.

So What's Next?

What can you do to support these women?

- Recognize that ADHD is a treatable medical condition managed through medication and therapy.

- Encourage the woman with ADHD and her family to work with a professional on recovery options. A good mental health professional can help find the best path to a healthy life.

- Do not attempt to offer treatment advice unless you have clinical training and experience diagnosing and treating mental illness.

- Be humble.

- Respect the woman's need to be alone and take care not to crowd her.

- Be nonjudgmental, and do not make assumptions about her competency, agency, or habits.

- Respect her wishes — she has a right to privacy, confidentiality, and dignity.

- Understand that she has a right to her thoughts and feelings without being judged by others.

- Do not demand perfection — do not shame or judge a woman with ADHD for lacking in certain areas.

- Treat her like you would want to be treated if you struggled in these areas.

- Accept the woman with ADHD for who she is and seek to understand her difficulties.

- Encourage her in the areas in which she has strengths, and to work on overcoming her weaknesses.

- Try to understand why she behaves the way that she does. She may have a good reason for doing something that seems inappropriate to you. It's important not to be judgmental.

- Do not ask her to thank you for understanding her or to show gratitude about accommodations made for her; this may make her resentful rather than grateful.

- Never ask a woman with ADHD to "try harder."

- Recognize that ADHD can affect all areas of her life, and she may need extra support in some areas.

- Understand that her lack of "normal" performance is not due to a lack of effort.

- A woman with ADHD needs to be supported in her efforts to manage her condition.

- Do not use shame, guilt, or fear to try to motivate her.

- You may feel frustrated at times with the woman who has ADHD, but you have no right to treat her badly because of that frustration.

- Try not to take ADHD personally and try to help others affected by the woman with ADHD's condition.

- Give her the benefit of the doubt and be understanding when she doesn't meet your expectations.

- Remember that a woman with ADHD may have trouble in school; it's important to remember that she

doesn't lack intelligence but simply operates differently to other students.

- Acknowledge that women with ADHD are often bril-
liant.

- Respect her privacy and do not judge her for doing
things differently to you.

- If a woman with ADHD needs extra time to complete
tasks, help her learn how to organize herself and be
productive in less time so she does not have to take on
more responsibilities than she can handle.

- Do not take responsibility for managing the symptoms
of ADHD yourself — rather, help the woman with
ADHD in managing them.

Women with ADHD can live productive and meaningful lives,
but they need support. The more educated we are about the
nature of ADHD in women, the better equipped we will be to
make wise choices and to support these women as necessary.

WOMEN WITH ADHD AND THE BUSI-
NESS WORLD

Women with ADHD can thrive in the business world just like men do. They may be very creative and innovative people who are good at coming up with new ideas — something rare among the population but very common among women with ADHD.

Women with ADHD can also be effective communicators, particularly when their priorities direct their communication style. Some are natural speakers who have a powerful way of getting their point across that is attractive to others. In contrast, others may not possess this natural speaking ability but can become excellent speakers with training or from practicing a lot. Women with ADHD who are uncomfortable in front of others can opt to study communication and presentation skills. They may also want to work with a coach or mentor who can help them improve their public-speaking skills and refine their communication styles.

Women with ADHD may be good at being assertive, just like many men are. However, instead of resorting to aggression as a way of expressing assertiveness, most women with ADHD are more likely to use an effective combination of logic and reason to argue their point when necessary.

They can also be very creative problem solvers who have their own unique style for solving problems that others may not be able to relate to. This makes them a natural fit for the business world.

Women with ADHD are generally quite loyal to those they care about and tend to be very compassionate toward others, which has makes it easy for them to build strong, long-lasting relationships.

Women with ADHD are generally very interesting people who can be inspirational to others with their energy and enthusiasm. This is particularly helpful in business as it makes them stand out from the crowd. They are often very good at energizing others and inspiring them through their enthusiasm for life. They are often great connectors that can facilitate connections between people, ideas, and strategies in a way that others may not be able to do.

"I Am Not a Career Woman"

Some women with ADHD have the false impression that they are not cut out to be career women because they have certain weaknesses. For example, some think this way because they have trouble managing time, organizing their paperwork neatly, or learning new skills quickly enough to perform certain jobs effectively — all problems commonly associated with adult ADHD.

However, the truth is that many women with ADHD are very good at managing their time and other organizational issues, which can make them great in a number of careers.

Women with ADHD sometimes think that being in a job where they have authority over others is just not for them. However, many women with ADHD can and do succeed in jobs with a great deal of authority over others.

Women also tend to be better at detail tasks than men, so there are very few jobs that men with ADHD can do as well as women with ADHD. Most men seem to be better at the big picture and strategic planning jobs, while women tend to be better at detail work. So, if you want a job that you can thrive in and excel at because of your innate strengths, choose a career path that gives you the opportunity to exercise your strengths.

Some women with ADHD assume that they can't afford to take jobs outside the home for various reasons. However, this isn't true if you have a family or dependents who will provide free childcare or give you flexible hours so you can pick up your children after school.

These generalizations are not carved in stone, but it's important to recognize that all women with ADHD have the chance to have a successful career.

CHAPTER 18: THE EFFECTS OF ADHD

Most women with ADHD experience a level of self-imposed guilt, shame, and remorse that doesn't happen as regularly when the disorder is found in males. They often feel obligated to apologize for their "stupid mistakes" even when they know no one is looking or holding them accountable. Even if the only person who knows they have ADHD is themselves, they may still feel ashamed about it. This can lead to severe anxiety, which can affect all aspects of one's life, from socializing to work performance.

DIVORCE, SEPARATION, AND LEGAL ISSUES

As we discussed earlier, women who suffer from ADHD are three times more likely than women without the disorder to divorce, and those who do divorce have more severe symptoms, such as depression. Divorced women with ADHD are also more likely to develop postpartum depression, which is when a woman becomes depressed after giving birth. Having ADHD itself is not a cause for divorce or separation; it only contributes to the stress and difficulty involved. However, many women with ADHD struggle with unmet expectations from both their partners and themselves. Partner abuse can also play a role in the breakdown of relationships.

Marriages between partners who both have ADHD are often more challenging than those involving only one with ADHD. These marriages can be extremely stressful and tumultuous, resulting in divorce. When children are involved, the struggles are often heightened and more difficult to navigate. When a woman struggles with ADHD, she may feel a sense of loss of control and anxiety, which can lead to serious depression.

Women with ADHD can also struggle with transmitting their anger, frustration, and disappointment to their partners either through vocal means or passive aggression. This can result in partners feeling unloved, unappreciated, or ignored by their wives, which can lead to serious marital problems and divorce.

To protect themselves legally, women with ADHD should do the following:

- Know their rights under the law before legal action is taken.

- Make sure that medical, legal, and other professionals have a clear understanding of their ADHD.

- Ask to see the written documentation of all evaluations and diagnoses used in the court system. Nothing should be left to chance.

- Obtain legal assistance if they wish to challenge custody awards or punitive custody rulings.

- Avoid being bullied or intimidated in the courtroom by speaking up for themselves and knowing their rights.

- Get advice and support from an attorney who is well-versed in ADHD.

- Seek out support groups who will either provide them with legal assistance or advise them on obtaining it.

- Be aware that even if they have been diagnosed with ADHD but have never taken medication or sought treatment, they can still be held liable for a child's neglect or abuse.

- Be aware that there is a lack of research on men and women with ADHD, leading to bias in the legal system. Women with ADHD are often unfairly accused of "abandoning" their children and their responsibilities because they have difficulty multitasking and concentrating. If this is happening to you, seek legal assistance right away.

- Be aware that there are no laws protecting women with ADHD who have difficulties functioning in the workforce. Women who are suffering from ADHD and are unable to work as a result of their symptoms are not covered by the Americans With Disabilities Act.

- Be aware that there are very few resources for women with ADHD and their families on the Internet, especially when considering the millions of people who might have this diagnosis. Many organizations help people with ADHD and their families, but few directories or online groups focus specifically on women with ADHD.

- Be aware that the legal system, doctors, psychologists, and other professionals are often not up to date on ADHD and thus do not know how to deal with it. This can lead to a lack of understanding regarding your options and treatment.

- Be aware that children will gain insight into ADHD and what drives their mother's behavior as they grow up. They will likely have questions about her medication, its effects on her, what the side effects are like, etc. It is critical that she spends as much time as possible explaining her ADHD, including how she feels when she misses doses. This will also help her children be more aware of how ADHD might impact their life.

- Be aware that there are a wide variety of options for legal assistance for women with ADHD. Legal assistance may be attained through government programs or non-profit foundations. These programs are designed to provide legal assistance to women with ADHD who would otherwise be unable to obtain it due to a lack of funds or insurance coverage, or simply because they are unsure where or how to seek help.

ADHD has become widely researched and recognized as a true medical condition in the past decade. However, in the legal field, it is still not widely accepted. Many judges, attorneys, and other professionals are still unaware of the effects of the disorder on women. Those who have been diagnosed but do not seek treatment for their symptoms and those women who have not even been diagnosed with ADHD can risk losing custody of their children or experiencing other unfortunate circumstances just because of their symptoms.

THE IMPACT OF ADHD ON CHILDREN

Children of ADHD women often suffer from various issues, including anxiety, aggression, grief and loss, developmental delays, defiance and disobedience, self-esteem issues, and many others. Research indicates that most children raised by an ADHD parent end up having such issues, especially if that parent is their mother. Depending on the child and their environment, these symptoms can manifest in a variety of ways and intensities. It is imperative that parents know the potential pitfalls and learn to recognize the symptoms early. Many adults who have a parent with untreated ADHD raised will recall their childhoods lacking structure or guidance. They often describe the chaos or lack of organization at home, which led to an increase in discipline issues and a sense of confusion regarding what was acceptable or "normal." Frequently, due to not having any guidance or direction in their childhoods, these children often become moody or depressed. When they are happy, they are often unable to reach out and share the joy they feel with others. This is often a result of a lack of social abilities and the confusion caused by their parent's ADHD symptoms. This can also lead to behaviors such as anger and temper tantrums.

THE ROLE OF MEDICAL ADVOCACY GROUPS IN FIGHTING ADHD

Although the term ADHD is not yet widely accepted in the legal field, many efforts are still being made to provide support and advocacy for adults with ADHD. Medical advocacy groups play an important role in providing direction and support to those diagnosed with ADHD but who have not received proper treatment for their disorder. They also provide information to other professionals about the symptoms of ADHD and how they interact with the body and mind. As a result, it has become more common for adults with this diagnosis to be taken more seriously.

Medical advocacy groups also provide methods for adults with ADHD to get medication without the expenses involved in obtaining a prescription. Many of these organizations also provide legal assistance for women with ADHD who have been charged with or wrongfully accused of abusing their children or spouses due to their symptoms. They also assist adults who have not yet been diagnosed but are seeking a diagnosis, which is particularly important because those who do not receive treatment are statistically more likely to act out in more severe ways.

Although ADHD is not yet widely accepted, it is no longer taboo to publicly discuss and be aware of the disorder. Awareness of this disorder has become more prevalent, leading professionals and the general public to understand that there are people who have untreated ADHD who may cause harm to themselves and others. Awareness is an important step in establishing a solid foundation for those affected by ADHD. Awareness will allow potential victims or offenders to seek guidance before making major decisions in their lives and futures.

Acknowledging an individual's condition can provide them with the opportunity to get the treatment that could potentially save their lives and shape a better future. By providing a guide on what to look for, how to handle it, and possible solutions to living with ADHD, sufferers will be better equipped when encountering a situation that doesn't have an immediate solution. Thanks to this increasing awareness, the public will be less likely to discriminate against individuals based on the actions or behavior caused by misdiagnosed symptoms, or those not recognized as symptoms due to lack of education. It is important to note that, along with raising awareness among the public, it is also important to raise awareness among lawmakers and other professionals.

Lack of awareness can lead to individuals being discriminated against, being denied jobs, housing, citizenship, and even being excluded from society.

CHAPTER 19: ADVICE FOR PARTNERS

Many women with ADHD share a common struggle: they feel particularly tired and overwhelmed once they've met their goal.

Ensuring your ADHD partner makes strides towards her professional and personal goals is imperative for maintaining long-term happiness and well-being. Below are ways to help make sure she gets the support she needs to stay balanced and feel good about her work.

1. Be a Source of Support

Even if your partner seems to have everything together on the outside, inside, she may be feeling stressed or frustrated and in need of encouragement from someone who understands what she's going through.

Consider speaking with your partner about handling the situation and discussing some positive things she can do to improve.

Should emotional support be an ongoing problem, consider joining a support group or therapy group with her (several options are available). This will allow you to be surrounded by people who understand what it's like to have ADHD, and it will also help your partner realize she isn't alone in her struggles.

2. Let Go of Guilt

Her ADHD symptoms are not her fault, nor is her fatigue.

Look at the bigger picture by reminding yourself that ADHD symptoms are physiological and can be managed with a combination of therapies and other interventions.

3. Understand the Importance of Mental Rest

Fatigue can be very draining, and your partner must regularly schedule mental rest to prevent stress overload. If she's feeling mentally drained or stressed, encourage her to tackle tasks when her brain is at its peak so she doesn't accumulate stress she can't handle. Fatigue and stress are often related—she may have trouble sleeping because her mind is still racing.

4. Schedule a Relaxing Break

Your partner will be more able to manage her fatigue and stress if she can take breaks in between challenging tasks.

Schedule regular breaks, even if it's just for a short period of time, to give her the mental rest she needs. When your partner is on a break from an activity or project, remind her that she can't work effectively until her brain has had time to relax and de-stress. Invite her to join you for a short walk, spend some time with friends or take a nap.

5. Consider Her Work/Life Balance

Many women with ADHD tend to have a difficult time maintaining an appropriate work/life balance because they are constantly busy and "on the go," and therefore may be less likely to take time for themselves.

Your partner must take time for herself, even if it's just 20 minutes each day. Often, small breaks throughout the day can lead to big improvements in mental focus and productivity. Suggest that she make a list of the things she enjoys doing most, whether it's taking a nap, shopping, or listening to music. Then help her create a schedule with these activities spaced out throughout the week so she can enjoy herself without overdoing it.

6. Take Her Out for a Treat

Your partner will likely find herself feeling tired and stressed out once she's accomplished a major work project or done something significant at school or work. Offer to take her out for a day, perhaps to an art gallery or museum. This will allow her brain to decompress from the rigors of work and school, giving it more time to rest and recharge before starting another project or intense activity.

7. Help Her with Meal Planning

Your partner with ADHD may not be very good at meal planning, and may require assistance in this area in order to maintain a healthy diet.

Consider going shopping together and helping her plan, prepare and cook meals. This can help her feel more in control of what she eats, and it will also be a great opportunity to bond with her over food. Once you've done that, help her stick to the meal schedule. Remind her that she needs to relax or socialize after dinner so that she can get a good night's rest.

8. Offer Her Healthy Snacks

Your partner needs to have healthy snacks on hand when hunger strikes. Buying healthy snacks can help her avoid snack cravings, leading to weight gain and unhealthy eating habits.

9. Avoid Stimulants and Sleep Deprivation

Stimulants such as coffee, energy drinks, cigarettes, or sodas are not the answer for long-term health, productivity or happiness. They can all have negative effects on ADHD symptoms, including fatigue and brain fog. A cup of coffee or energy drink may give your partner a temporary burst of energy, but they also mess with her brain chemistry in the long run.

Sleep deprivation can also affect your partner's health and productivity, and it may worsen her ADHD symptoms. Encourage her to sleep as much as she can, especially when she is feeling fatigued. If she's not sleeping enough at night, encourage her to nap in the afternoon. When she naps, have a designated time that is quiet and dark, so she doesn't disturb herself with noise or light.

10. Have Her Make a List of Activities She Enjoys Doing

Your partner will probably have a huge list of things she enjoys doing, and once you know what they are, you can plan to do these activities .

For example, she might enjoy walking outdoors and going to the beach. Or she might enjoy gardening or volunteering at a local animal shelter. Encourage your partner to choose one or two of these activities to do each week.

11. Suggest That She Sleep in a Dark Room

Your partner's bedroom should be dark to encourage sleep and prevent her from being disturbed by noise or light during the night. It should also be comfortable and conducive to sleep. The room should be quiet, have no outside distractions, and there should be nothing in it that will cause her to feel anxious or upset.

If at all possible, your partner should remove all electronic devices such as clocks, fans, radios, and televisions from her bedroom because the light coming from them can wake her up when she's trying to go to sleep at night. These lights can also cause her problems with ADHD by keeping her brain active, thus preventing a good night's sleep.

12. Encourage Her to Exercise Regularly

Exercise is vital for the health and well-being of your partner with ADHD. Encourage her to exercise regularly alongside you or with a friend, family member, or coworker. This will allow her to expend excess energy and regain mental and physical stamina, which will help her manage her ADHD symptoms.

13. Help Your Partner Learn About Nutrition

Many people with ADHD are unaware of their nutritional needs, food allergies and sensitivities.

Encourage your partner to read as much as she can about proper nutrition and its role in her overall health. The more she understands food, the more likely she will be to choose foods that will promote healthy brain function.

14. Reward Your Partner for Positive Behavior

Your partner with ADHD can be very hard on herself when things don't go well. Encourage her to make a list of all of her good behaviors and reward her with small treats like movie tickets, a massage, or a shopping spree if she accomplishes something you approve of.

Encourage her to keep track of all of the things she does for her family and friends that are positive or supportive. This will help her realize that it is not just what she does but also who she is that makes a difference in people's lives. It will also remind her to think about how she can influence others without overdoing it and causing herself harm.

MANAGING MEDICATION

Once your partner gets her ADHD under control, she will likely have to take one or more medications to manage. There are some things you can do to make sure she takes this medication as prescribed and feels as well as possible. Here are some tips:

1. Get Your Partner's Medications Organized

Your partner should have her medications well-organized so she knows where they are at all times and remembers to take them at the right time.

Your partner will probably want to keep her medication in a place that is not too accessible, especially if she has children or pets. However, she should make sure that the medication is in plain view so that if she has any questions about what it is or what it does, she can see it and read the instructions.

2. Ask Your Partner Whether or Not She Feels Overmedicated

Medication can be different for everybody. For example, some people feel extremely happy and upbeat when they are on medication for ADHD, while others feel completely drugged out. Ask your partner whether or not she feels like she is overmedicated and if it bothers her. If so, tell her that you will be supportive of whatever decision she makes to manage her symptoms in future.

3. Help Your Partner Discontinue Medications That Are No Longer Beneficial

There are many medications that are no longer used for treating ADHD because they are ineffective or even dangerous to use for long periods of time. If your partner is on one of these medications, tell her that you will be supportive of her if she decides to stop taking it. You can mention the benefit of using a medication that has been researched and approved for treating ADHD, as well as any potential negative side effects.

4. Help Your Partner Understand Side Effects

If your partner is experiencing side effects from her medication, it is important that she understands them as soon as possible so that she can take steps to help mitigate them in an effective way. If she feels uncomfortable with the side effects, she might be interested in switching medications.

5. Let Her Make Her Own Decisions Regarding Medication

Your partner might feel too much pressure to take her medication if you are strongly encouraging her to do so. Rather than putting pressure on her, ask her what she thinks about taking the medication and how she feels about it. Then, without pressuring her, inquire about how you can assist her. This way, your partner will feel like the decision is in her hands, which is empowering for anyone.

6. Be Supportive of Your Partner's Decision to Stop Taking Medication

Many people decide to stop taking medication because they feel that they have become dependent on it. If your partner is feeling this way, support her decision and try to understand her reasons for stopping. For example, she might believe that the medicine is not helping her in any way and that she feels like a better version of herself without it. If so, it is up to you to support her through the process of stopping the medication.

CHAPTER 20: TRANSITIONING TO ADULTHOOD WITH ADHD

For some people, the transition from adolescence to adulthood is difficult. When entering this new stage of life, there are so many things to consider that it can be overwhelming. Just like in childhood and adolescence, many environmental factors play a role in how our lives proceed into adulthood. These include parents, peers, and other family members.

As women who have ADHD become adults, they may have to meet many new responsibilities and cope with the changes that these shifts can wreak. They will have to make decisions about their future. They will have to confront a variety of stressors, including issues related to money, work, time spent at home with children, and family dynamics.

These are all things that women with ADHD tend to struggle with. Individuals with ADHD generally do not adapt as well to rapid changes in their schedules and circumstances. As a result, when a big change occurs for them such as job loss or divorce, they often feel even more lost and confused than people without ADHD.

Adult women with ADHD often have more difficulty graduating from college and finding jobs than their male counterparts, according to the National Institute of Mental Health. They also have elevated stress levels and rates of divorce, depression, and drug abuse compared to those without ADHD.

As they get older, it is common for women with ADHD to develop other health problems. These include thyroid disease, diabetes, sleep disorders, and cardiovascular disease. All of these can be resolved by combining medication and behavioral changes.

Many women with ADHD try to find ways of coping with their symptoms by themselves. When these attempts fail, they will often see a doctor and seek treatment. However, many women do not choose to consult a doctor because they are unaware that they have ADHD in the first place. This is one of the reasons why it is very important for doctors, educators, coaches, and other professionals that work with women to know how to spot the symptoms and refer them for assessment if necessary.

Let's recap some of the ways to identify ADHD in adult women to make the process easier for everyone involved:

- Repeatedly missing appointments and forgetting things.

- Not having a strong work ethic, meaning they often fail to complete projects that they start.

- Being excessively fidgety and constantly interrupting others with excessive talking, squirming on seats, pacing back and forth, etc.

- Excessive response in the form of over-blowing issues (i.e. excessive anger towards a particular issue), a negative attitude being loudly expressed, or not being able to keep one's cool when faced with something that triggers an emotional reaction such as sadness or anger.

- Excessive over-thinking (worrying about things that are not a problem).

- Irritating others with excessive compliments, criticism and frequently using pet names when referring to others.

- Being very bossy, demanding, and domineering over others in relationships.

- Excessive talking in meetings without contributing much to the discussion.

- The tendency to engage in power struggles and not being able to give up the lead when it is time for others to take turns.

- Being easily agitated, irritable and quick to anger.

- Needing more frequent reminders about things than others do, or being unable to follow through with assigned tasks despite being reminded several times already.

- Losing track of conversations because of inattention or constantly interrupting others by speaking about unimportant topics.

- Having trouble managing the time allocated to them by over-committing to things or procrastinating because of difficulty organizing tasks and planning.

- Being prone to impulsive spending, binge eating, shopping sprees, and other types of unregulated spending behaviors due to the reduced ability to think ahead and do long-term planning.

- Being flirtatious with others to seek attention or feel

good about themselves. This often leads to short-term relationships that don't last as long as they otherwise might because they cannot commit to one person for any length of time.

These symptoms can be identified by asking the right questions and observing body language. For example, when someone who does not have ADHD is told about a topic of interest, she will typically listen carefully and eagerly focus all of her attention on the topic at hand without being easily distracted by anything else around her. The person with ADHD will often daydream or look around at things that are not relevant to the conversation. She will also fidget or tap her fingers as if she is waiting for something.

In addition to the physical characteristics listed above that indicate ADHD symptoms in women, it's important to be aware of other medical conditions that may coexist.

PART 5 - FUTURE PROSPECTS FOR WOMEN WITH ADHD

CHAPTER 21: ADHD'S ROLE IN THE EVOLVING LANDSCAPE OF MEDICAL ADVANCEMENTS IN THE NEXT DECADE

How will things change for women with ADHD in this century? What can we expect from future treatment?

For starters, we can expect to see a much greater divide between men and women regarding diagnosis rates. This is because while boys are still over-diagnosed with ADHD, girls are more likely to be chronically undiagnosed — meaning they'll have been diagnosed with inattentive-type symptoms but never receive an ADHD diagnosis. We might also start seeing more of a divide between younger kids who've been diagnosed poorly and older kids who have had their diagnosis corrected.

More importantly, we might also see more research focusing on ADHD as a gender-specific disorder in women. Women with ADHD have been largely ignored and marginalized in research, so this would be a significant step forward. For example, in the 1970s and 1980s, many of the diagnostic manuals considered ADHD irrelevant to women, which meant that clinicians didn't think about it when treating female patients. Even when the DSM-III came out in 1980, it only included a separate "subgroup" diagnosis for women. Women with ADHD were finally given attention in 1994 when the DSM-IV was published, and ADHD was included in Section III (Abnormal Involuntary Actions and Their Consequences).

The gender divide will also be driven by a greater understanding of how female brains respond to stimulants in particular. As more research is done, we might find that the same brain abnormalities arise in women with ADHD as in men — and that they need to be treated with the same drugs. This might mean that women and men will shortly receive equal treatment for their ADHD.

These changes will undoubtedly benefit women with attention problems, but other aspects of ADHD's future are still up in the air. For example, we still don't know enough about the diagnosis or treatment of childhood ADHD in girls or the effects gender has on ADHD symptoms in adulthood. And although it's estimated that up to one in seven adults falls into the severe ADHD spectrum, we still don't know the long-term impact of ADHD on adults or exactly how many women and men have this diagnosis.

So, what can we learn from the previous half-century of research? First, we've learned that it's crucial not to overlook childhood symptoms and that many cases do respond well to medication. We also know more about the role of families in the development of ADHD and how parenting styles affect children's responses to medicine. Finally, we know that ADHD is a global disorder that requires awareness of cultural differences and their impact on diagnostic procedures.

Again, these things will become clearer over time, so we can't say for certain what's ahead for women with ADHD. But if we consider the trend that began in the 1950s, the future isn't looking bleak for the next generation of ladies with attention disorders.

THE FUTURE OF ADHD

There are two schools of thought when it comes to the future of ADHD. The first says that ADHD is on the rise, and we'll continue diagnosing more people with it. According to the second school of thought, overdiagnosis of ADHD is already occurring and will level off in the near future. The reality, however, is that it's hard to predict anything at all. The truth is likely somewhere in between.

We know that ADHD is still largely underrecognized as a serious medical condition and relatively unrecognized as a global disorder. It may indeed become more common over time — possibly because both kids and adults are getting better at recognizing this disorder — but it's important to remember that it's still quite rare today.

In other words, many women have yet to be diagnosed with ADHD and find themselves struggling in a world where symptoms like forgetfulness and distractibility are considered negative personality traits rather than medical conditions. It's hard to say what a world with better recognition for ADHD will look like, as we don't have enough data. But if we look at the past half-century of ADHD research, it seems likely that there will always be an overdiagnosis problem and that women won't be afforded equal treatment until this issue is cleared up.

Looking ahead, it's clear that doctors and researchers will devote more time and resources to diagnosing and treating ADHD.

They'll continue working on new diagnostic tools, such as video games that can test a person's symptoms, and studying the long-term effects of medications on women with ADHD.

We might also see a number of changes in how ADHD is defined and classified in the future, creating new subgroups for men and women. This could allow for better recognition of gender-specific symptoms.

This is a lot of work to be done, and there are still many unanswered questions. For example, we don't know the best age to start taking medication or if they affect women differently to men. As such, we should expect much more research in the future on both of these topics — especially since ADHD research funding has increased dramatically over the past decade.

CHAPTER 22: WOMEN'S CONTRIBUTION TO ADRESSING ADHD ISSUES

Y ou can do a lot to help yourself and others with ADHD, especially if you work together as a team. Understanding and accepting ADHD as a medical condition can make coping with this disorder much easier for everyone involved. You can also use the many ADHD resources for women that are available. And if you have children suffering from ADHD, you must understand what steps need to be taken for proper diagnosis and treatment. And as moms, sisters, girlfriends, or partners to men or women with ADHD, your role is extremely important because you have the ability to create a strong team around someone with attention problems — whether they're your husband or wife or one of your friends or family members.

Women with ADHD can change the world, just as men can. They have the same potential for success and personal fulfillment that men do. Beyond that, ADHD women bring valuable perspectives to the table — whether they're trying to advance in a male-dominated profession or running their own businesses while also maintaining households and raising families. But they also face unique challenges because of gender expectations — how they're supposed to look, act, and speak based on their biology. It's important that you understand these issues in order to be happy and successful in whatever role you have in life.

ADHD women are now leading a highly visible and successful charge to get recognition for this disorder. There are many proactive organizations, government agencies, and charities established by women with ADHD. As more people become aware of the disorder and recognize its unique characteristics in females, we can expect a greater increase in awareness of women with ADHD.

With such revolutionary changes on the horizon, it's important to pay attention to the issues facing women with ADHD today. Problems with social standing and self-confidence can happen whether your disease is mild or severe. The more knowledge you gain about ADHD, the more control you'll have over your life, giving you the freedom to live a happy, productive life on your own terms. Simultaneously, you can assist others by setting a positive example that you can be proud of.

If you have ADHD, you have talents and gifts. They may appear in areas such as brainstorming, inventing and problem-solving, creativity (music, art, architecture), entrepreneurship, leadership abilities, business, and financial skills. Many of these are the same characteristics that typify great leaders in other areas as well.

Women with ADHD often put a high value on family life. They want to be good wives and good mothers — but they often struggle with holding down a regular job. With their powerful drive for achievement and perfectionism keeping them from reaching career goals or fulfilling their responsibilities at home, women with ADHD are sometimes seen as irresponsible or immature. But they are usually quite the opposite.

SUPPORT NETWORKING FOR WOMEN WITH ADHD

As a growing population of women and girls are diagnosed with ADHD, the need for greater awareness and understanding is essential. But in today's world, support networks for women with ADHD are just starting to take shape.

Some doctors, psychologists, and psychiatrists have opened specialized ADHD practices for women and girls. Others have established private practices that treat both men and women with ADHD together. Some non-profit organizations provide seminars and roundtables dealing with ADHD, specifically in females. And several groups devoted specifically to female professionals also address issues related to adult ADHD.

However, many women with ADHD are still having a hard time getting the support they need. Many of them feel that they have been "failed" by the medical community, and they turn to each other for help instead. These self-help groups usually provide forums for swapping tips about coping mechanisms as well as validating experiences and frustrations.

Several ADHD-specific digital communities have formed on social media platforms to address this need for support. Many of these include posting positive messages, sharing inspirational stories and experiences, asking experts questions, and receiving feedback from other women with ADHD. These websites can be a valuable resource for anyone looking for ADHD information and resources.

Despite all that has been accomplished, there is still much room for improvement. The number of women — and girls — diagnosed with ADHD continues to grow every year. In addition, many women with ADHD are unable to find a work-life balance or success in traditional careers. These problems will continue until society comes up with new ways to help ADHD sufferers get through everyday life more smoothly.

This is a call to action. More women and girls have ADHD than ever before. The worldwide rate of ADHD in women is about 10%. This translates to approximately 8 million females of all ages in the United States, currently suffering from the disorder. This figure excludes those who have been misdiagnosed or who have not received a proper diagnosis.

However, many myths and misconceptions about ADHD in women still exist, making it difficult to receive a diagnosis or treatment, let alone gain acceptance from employers or coworkers.

Women with ADHD have the power and skills to change their lives now and create a more balanced future for themselves and future generations, while there is still much progress to be made.

There is hope for finding better ways to handle the challenges of living with ADHD. As more people become aware of the disorder and its symptoms, women will have better access to the information they need and a greater ability make an accurate diagnosis or seek treatment.

In time, we will see a greater understanding of gender differences in this complex condition, resulting in better access to care and treatments that work effectively for women with ADHD.

CONCLUSION

I nitially, ADHD was observed mainly in boys and men, but now it has been found in girls and women too. The concomitant development of ADHD in males and females indicates that there are biological factors involved, as well as environmental ones. However, the exact effect of these factors is still unclear, particularly in girls and women. Most of them do not have as much external ADHD behavior as males.

In order to truly understand the prevalence of ADHD in women and girls, it is important to analyze the impact of gender on the development, presentation, and treatment of the condition. In recent years, more clinical trials have focused on gender-based differentiations. Studies show that women may require fewer stimulants, and may need to monitor medication side effects more closely than males. Gender has proven to be a crucial factor in evaluating ADHD.

ADHD affects women differently than men because they have different gender roles, different parenting styles, and a different sense of being competent at work compared to men. Girls with ADHD may be more self-conscious about negative or problematic behaviors such as hyperactivity, impulsivity and inattention. ADHD in females can be the cause of low self-esteem, problems with relationships, depression, eating disorders, and drug abuse.

However, there are numerous treatments available to address the issue, including individual, group, and other types of psychological therapies. As part of ADHD awareness projects, some school interventions are also available. Doctors and psychiatrists can provide many different types of medications that may help girls and women with ADHD. The best treatment depends on various factors such as the severity of symptoms, availability and access to resources, personal preferences, and their impact on daily life.

Therapies such as psychoeducation, behavior therapy, and contingency management are often used to treat girls and women with ADHD.

There are many myths about women and girls with ADHD which contribute to the fact that they are often left undiagnosed or untreated. It is important that people who deal with these women on a daily basis help them without making them self-conscious or offending them.

Women have many ways of adapting to life with ADHD, but they regularly face problems with self-esteem issues, relationships, school, and jobs. The easiest solution for women is one of acceptance and support provided by friends, loved ones, and family members.

Women should feel confident in themselves and know that their ADHD is not their fault. This should make us think twice before making a judgment. We must understand that all of us have our own different ways of managing our unique challenges, so people with ADHD should not be judged; it is the same as judging someone because he/she is left-handed.

We need to be more aware of the impact of ADHD on girls and women in order to do further research and develop appropriate treatments. The emotional support of family members, friends, and coworkers is extremely important because no one has ADHD on purpose, and everyone needs assistance in order to overcome their challenges.

The improvement of life quality of girls and women with ADHD can be achieved with proper education and support from all sides, including the media, families, teachers, employers, and institutions. This way we can create good communication between all parties involved. This will help girls and women with ADHD to feel comfortable in their own skin, and feel happy and healthy, which is the most important thing.